What People Are Saying About
Chicken Soup for the Teenage Soul Letters . . .

"I really enjoyed reading the letters in this book. I have gone through a lot in the past two years, but reading these letters made me feel like I will get through it all and might even be a better person because of what I've been through."

Theresa, 16

"The letters in this book really made me see how great my family and friends are. I am going to start writing letters to the people I love to tell them how much I appreciate them."

Jamie, 15

"I love all the *Chicken Soup* books, but I enjoyed this one the most. I felt like I was one step closer to the magic that makes these books so loved by teens. It was like I had a special 'back-stage pass' that allowed me to see into the inner workings of these books and their readers."

Melissa, 18

"I can't explain the way this book made me feel. It was even better than the 'regular' *Chicken Soup* books because the stories and letters were so personal and uplifting. The Tough Stuff section was incredibly sad, but it made me realize how blessed I am and how every moment is precious. I hope you continue to share these letters and stories with us."

Kristi, 15

"I want to thank you for continuing to believe in us (teens) by doing these books. What I loved about this book was that it felt like I could have written many of the stories and letters myself. That made me feel so good because I felt like I am important and I matter (well, at least to people like you, Jack and Mark). Thanks so very much. You make me feel good about being a teen."

Lisa, 14

"The *Chicken Soup for the Soul* books have been some of the best books I have ever read. Knowing that everyday people contribute some of their real-life, personal stories to these books makes a huge impact on myself as the reader."

Gina, 16

"Being a teen with a disability is not easy, no matter how you look at it. However, reading this book did so much to ease the pain and change my perspective that I am honestly grateful for my situation now. This is the first time I have seen the blessings instead of just the difficulties of my disabilities."

Chris, 18

"I have two teenage daughters who love *Chicken Soup for the Teenage Soul*. I always read a few stories before passing the books on to my daughters. I could not put this one down. I was so intrigued by the teens, teachers and parents who wrote in. I found it to be absolutely spellbinding. I think it is a shame that more parents won't know to read this book before giving it to their teens."

Terry, mother of two

"After reading this book I look at my life with a positive new perspective. It affected my relationships with friends, family and even myself."

Jenny, 15

"I've always wondered what the other people who read these books are like. Now I know—they're just like me."

Catherine, 16

"This is a great book. I have been feeling pretty down lately, so it was nice to know that others have gone through similar times in their lives. It takes a lot to share something so personal, so I really appreciate that the writers in this book were so honest and open. This book makes me feel like I'm not alone."

Kerry, 17

CHICKEN SOUP
FOR THE
TEENAGE SOUL
LETTERS

Letters of Life,
Love and Learning

Jack Canfield
Mark Victor Hansen
Kimberly Kirberger

Health Communications, Inc.
Deerfield Beach, Florida

www.hci-online.com
www.chickensoup.com
www.teenagechickensoup.com

We would like to acknowledge the following publishers and individuals for permission to reprint the following material. (Note: The stories that were penned anonymously, that are public domain, or that were written by Jack Canfield, Mark Victor Hansen or Kimberly Kirberger are not included in this listing.)

Healing Words. Reprinted by permission of Corey Dweck. ©2001 Corey Dweck.

Thanks, Mom! Reprinted by permission of Rebecca Kross. ©1998 Rebecca Kross.

My Sister's First Love. Reprinted by permission of Kristi Vesterby. ©1999 Kristi Vesterby.

Immortal. Reprinted by permission of Jodi Vesterby. ©1999 Jodi Vesterby.

Unconditional Love. Reprinted by permission of Rachel Palmer. ©1999 Rachel Palmer.

Guy Repellent. Reprinted by permission of Erin Seto. ©1999 Erin Seto.

Always a Tomorrow and *My Letter.* Reprinted by permission of Ashley Lusk. ©2001 Ashley Lusk.

April 15, the Worst and Best Day of My Life. Reprinted by permission of Laurel Walker. ©1999 Laurel Walker.

(Continued on page 322)

Library of Congress Cataloging-in-Publication Data

Chicken soup for the teenage soul letters : letters of life, love, and learning / [compiled by] Jack Canfield, Mark Victor Hansen, Kimberly Kirberger.
    p. cm.
  ISBN 1-55874-805-9 (hardcover) — ISBN 1-55874-804-0 (trade paper)
  1. Teenagers—Conduct of life.   I. Canfield, Jack, date.   II. Hansen, Mark Victor, date.   III. Kirberger, Kimberly, date.

BJ1661 .C45 2001
158.1'28'0835—dc21   00-053614

©2001 Jack Canfield and Mark Victor Hansen
ISBN 1-55874-804-0 (trade paper) ISBN 1-55874-805-9 (hardcover)

Publisher: Health Communications, Inc.
           3201 S.W. 15th Street
           Deerfield Beach, FL 33442-8190

Cover re-design by Andrea Perrine Brower
Typesetting by Lawna Patterson Oldfield

With love, we dedicate this to
all the teenagers who have written
to thank us and to share
their stories.

We thank you for wanting
to help and inspire
your fellow teens.

Contents

1. DEAR CHICKEN SOUP . . .

2. OVERCOMING OBSTACLES

3. THANK YOU!

4. INSIGHTS AND LESSONS

5. TOUGH STUFF

6. HELPING OTHERS

Acknowledgments

This book is a compilation of the thousands of thank-yous we have received since the release of the first *Chicken Soup for the Teenage Soul* book. First and foremost, we want to thank all of the teens, teachers and parents who took the time to sit down and write us a thank-you letter. Each and every one of them meant the world to us and they continue to be the fuel that allows us to compile these books with total dedication to you.

We thank Lia Gay for being the teenager she "was," for being open-hearted enough to have a friendship with an ADULT, for being articulate enough to express accurately the angst of teens and for picking up (and reading) *Chicken Soup for the Soul* every time she came over. All of this, combined with our love for her, resulted in the decision to do a *Chicken Soup* book for TEENS . . . wow!!!!

We thank the ones we love for loving us back and nurturing our souls and hearts so sweetly: Inga Mahoney,

Patti Hansen, Johnny Anderson, Christopher, Kyle, Oran, Jesse, Elizabeth and Melanie.

Mitch Claspy is someone who I (Kim) cannot thank enough but I won't ever stop trying. He is the most loyal, committed, focused, (cute), honorable and together person I know and *I thank him* from the bottom of my heart for everything he does and will continue to do. This book is in your hands because of his hard work and dedication to teens. I feel blessed to have a friend like Mitch. I am so lucky to work with people I love. Mitch, wipe that smirk off your face and just say, "Thanks."

Tasha Boucher is just plain amazing. She worked so hard on this book. She called and researched and interviewed and called again. She has notes that if stacked up would be as tall as my house and each one of them was something important to her because it would help you or inspire you. Whenever given the opportunity to take the easy road or the road that will inspire or nurture you, she, without question, takes the difficult one. That alone would be more than enough, but she also is the biggest and most precious support system I have. Everyone should be so lucky as to have a friend like her.

A big thanks to Nina Palais who runs the Teen Letter Project with such grace. Because of her, every letter we receive is read and answered. It is that dedication that has helped to make this book a reality. Thank you, Nina, for your friendship and your kind spirit.

Kelly Harrington works very hard to attain permission to print all the letters in this book. We are deeply grateful to Kelly for her commitment and focus.

Thanks to Lisa Wood-Vasquez who does an amazing job as Kim's assistant. She always has a positive attitude. We thank her for her sense of humor and her ability to put so much care into all she does. She is a pleasure to work (and walk) with.

There is no way we could have dreamed of doing this book without our remarkable staff of teens. They read all the letters we receive, give their feedback and recommendations on every submission and infuse the entire process with their positive energy. We thank the following teens for their brilliance: Christine Kalinowski, Hayley Gibson, Jenny Sharaf, Ashley Fisher, Dawn Geer, Rose Lannutti and Arianna Axelrod.

We thank our publisher, Peter Vegso, who has kept the *Teenage Soul* dream alive by continuing to believe in these books.

Patty Aubery, you are amazing. You do the work of five people and still manage to be the coolest person we know.

Heather McNamara and D'ette Corona did an awesome job of putting together the final manuscript of this book. Their brilliant editing skills and creative feedback were invaluable to the process and for that we thank them both.

The following people read the original manuscript and gave their feedback on how to make the book better. We are deeply grateful for their collective wisdom. A warm thank you to: Julia House, Katie Conner, Erin Downey, Lisa Siciliano, Sarah Dawn Swicegood, Michelle Andoniello, Berni Donovan, Samuel Schultz, Caitlin Hart, Loren Robeck, Mara Mirus, Lauren Mee, Anna Meyer, Katrina Mumaw, Meghan Deppenschmidt, Kelly Kitts, Denise Kitts, Lauri Engman, Emily Pember, Laura Bauer, Pamela Rizzo, Jennifer Kirkland, Sara Alamdar, Amanda McKinney, Christina Peltier, Tara Brandenburger, Britney Graham, Karen Groth, Cary McCormick, Rose Lannutti, Dawn Geer, Christine Alvarez, Rebecca Woolf, Lisa Rothbard, Kelly Harrington, Christine Kalinowski, Hayley Gibson and Jenny Sharaf.

Thanks to Colin Mortensen for being a great friend to Kim and Jesse, and an inspirational speaking partner.

Sharon House has done a wonderful job of promoting this book and getting it into as many hands as possible. We appreciate every effort she has made on this book's behalf. Thank you, Sharon.

Nancy Autio is always there for us and gave us amazing feedback and support throughout the process of putting this book together. Thank you, Nancy, for being so fun to work with.

The entire staff of Jack Canfield's and Mark Victor Hansen's offices—Nancy Autio, Leslie Riskin, Teresa Esparza, Veronica Romero, Robin Yerian, Cindy Holland, Vince Wong, Sarah White, Deborah Hatchell, Patty Hansen, Trudy Marschall, Maria Nickless, Laurie Hartman, Michelle Adams, Tracy Smith, Dee Dee Romanello, Joy Pieterse, Lisa Williams, Kristi Knopp and David Coleman—did an incredible job of keeping everything together during the production of this book. They work so hard and we love and appreciate each and every one of them.

Our brilliant editors at Health Communications, Inc., Lisa Drucker and Susan Tobias, have done everything humanly possible to make this a great book. They are both so wise and talented (and patient) and we adore them.

Kim Weiss is a great friend, who also happens to be our talented publicist at Health Communications, Inc. Kim, you are a pleasure to work with.

Kimberley Denney and Maria Dinoia of Health Communications, Inc. also do an excellent job of keeping the *Chicken Soup* books on the bestseller lists with their publicity efforts. You are so appreciated.

Randee Feldman, *Chicken Soup for the Soul* product manager at Health Communications, Inc., has been a great support of and advocate for our projects.

Terry Burke and Kelly Maragni of Health Communications, Inc. have done a masterful job at selling and marketing the *Chicken Soup* books.

Thanks to Andrea Perrine Brower and Lawna Patterson Oldfield at Health Communications, Inc. for the inspiring and creative design efforts on this book.

We also thank other *Chicken Soup* coauthors: Raymond Aaron, Patty and Jeff Aubery, Nancy Autio, Marty Becker, Ron Camacho, Tim Clauss, Barbara DeAngelis, Mark and Chrissy Donnelly, Irene Dunlop, Patty Hansen, Jennifer Read Hawthorne, Carol Kline, Hanoch and Meladee McCarty, Heather McNamara, Maida Rogerson, Martin Rutte, Marci Shimoff, Barry Spilchuk and Diana von Welanetz Wentworth.

Our warm and loving gratitude for everyone who made this book possible. We love each and every one of you.

Introduction

To send a letter is a good way to go some-where without moving anything but your heart.

Phyllis Theroux

Dear Teens,

In 1997 we released the first *Chicken Soup* book written especially for teens. Since that time we have been deeply moved by your responses to the books, especially in the form of letters you have written to us. Your letters have been filled with heartfelt thank-yous and detailed descriptions of how a particular story or stories helped you and gave you a newfound faith in the process of life.

When I was interviewed for the book, I remember saying many times that this generation—so often accused of being selfish and ill-mannered—took the time to sit down and write beautifully articulate thank-you letters. I, a generally grateful person, had never done the same and I wanted people to know how kind and thoughtful this generation is—despite what many would have us believe.

These thank-you letters continued to pour in and we found that reading them brought us even closer to teens and to the issues they were dealing with. More often than not, the letters were as personal and as insightful as the stories they were thanking us for. Some of the letters were so honest and revealing that the teenagers on our staff were compelled to write their own personal letters in response.

Now that there are a total of five *Chicken Soup* books for your age group—*Chicken Soup for the Teenage Soul I, II, III, Journal* and *College Soul*—this phenomenon only continues to grow. More and more we find ourselves telling each other that we should do a book of "the stories behind the stories."

Many of you have written to us asking, "What happened to Lia Gay? Is she still in love?" or, "How is Mike doing? Do you ever hear from him?" Because many of the contributors have their contact information in the back of the book, they receive letters personally from the teens who were particularly touched or changed by their story. More than once the writers have told us that they received a thank-you from a reader at a time when they were doubting their own worth or struggling with their own issues, and the thank-you letter came at the perfect moment.

The main reason we were compelled to share this book with you is because we want to share the caring and generosity that continues after the books are read. When we first used the slogan "Teens Helping Teens," we couldn't have dreamed of the enormity of that statement.

It is very important to us that as you read these stories and letters you understand that we are very clear about where the credit belongs for all of this. You the reader, you the teenager, you the one who opened up your heart either to help or to be helped, are the ones responsible for this. You, the teens who shared the deepest part of yourselves, who with trust and great hope looked for an answer, you with a heart full of gratitude who wrote us a thank-you, and you, who cared about people you didn't even know and wrote to us to find out how they were doing. You are the ones who have created this cycle of love and healing.

It is our deepest hope that the healing continue and that you, the reader, know how incredibly grateful we are for being a part of and being able to continue nurturing this community of teens helping teens.

This book is for you!

With great love,

Kim, Jack and Mark

Healing Words

When I'm feeling all alone,
A stranger from the group
I pour myself a heaping bowl
Of Teenage Chicken Soup.

Those I meet inside here
Never ask me to explain.
They understand without a word
And also feel my pain.

Was it something in my story
That changed your life today?
The healing words of one like me
Who found himself astray?

Did you feel that bond between us
Through our taking and our giving?
Did you touch that part inside my heart
That said to go on living?

Your words come flying back to me.
They lay upon your letter.
I'm glad to know I helped you
And that you're feeling better.

When you are feeling stronger
Since our lives and words have crossed
Go out and help another soul
Who's out there feeling lost.

Corey Dweck

Share with Us

We would love to hear your reactions to the letters in this book and the stories in all the other *Chicken Soup for the Soul* books. Please let us know what your favorite stories were and how they affected you.

We also invite you to send us letters and stories you would like to see published in future editions of *Chicken Soup for the Teenage Soul*. Please send submissions to:

Chicken Soup for the Teenage Soul Letters
P.O. Box 936
Pacific Palisades, CA 90272
Fax: 805-563-2945
e-mail: *stories@Iam4teens.com*

Come visit our Web site:
www.teenagechickensoup.com

You can also visit the *Chicken Soup for the Soul* site at:
www.chickensoup.com

We hope you enjoy reading this book as much as we enjoyed compiling, editing and writing it.

1

DEAR CHICKEN SOUP...

The most beautiful thing in the world is, precisely, the conjunction of learning and inspiration.

Wanda Landowska

Thanks, Mom!

Dear Chicken Soup,

I want to thank you for your book *Chicken Soup for the Teenage Soul*. I have never read a book that made me cry so hard. I probably could relate to 97 percent of the stories.

I am a senior in high school. For four years I have been a member of the marching band at my school—four years of commitment to an organization of 150 kids, four teachers and 100 parents working from August to June of every school year. For four years, my mom has been there for me—never complaining, and never receiving a "Thanks, Mom." My mother is pretty much a supermom and, unfortunately, it took me some seventeen years to realize it.

"Chauffeur" is probably a more appropriate name

for her. Every concert, every competition, every football game, my mom was there with a smile. She always stayed to watch—even through the football games. And when she couldn't be there, my mom would be waiting for me when the bus pulled into the school's parking lot.

The strange thing is, my mother actually enjoyed arriving at the school at 10:30 at night just for me to tell her that I was going out with my friends and that I needed twenty dollars instead of a ride home. She enjoyed selling cowbells and blankets, seat cushions and tickets—just as long as I was happy. Now that I'm a senior, I have my own car and drive myself to my football games and concerts. My mother still comes to watch me.

Recently, my band was invited to play for the fiftieth anniversary celebration of ETS (Educational Testing Service). When the bus pulled up to the flagpole in front of my high school I had the strangest feeling. Something was missing. I found myself desperately searching for my mom in the parking lot. I needed to tell her I didn't need a ride home; I was going out. I then realized my mother was at home and probably in bed. I never realized how much I took her for granted until she wasn't there.

When I got home that night, I woke her up and told her I loved her and I missed her. I told my mom that I really appreciated all the times she had driven my friends and me back and forth and around the world. I told her I was glad she embarrassed me all those times, because I knew that it just meant she loved me, too. My mom looked back at me with tears and a big smile.

Thank you for the wonderful books! They have inspired me to show my gratitude and my love to the people who matter. My mom thanks you, as well.

Sincerely,

Rebecca Kross

My Sister's First Love

Dear Chicken Soup for the Teenage Soul,

I am sending you a story my sister wrote for your consideration for a *Chicken Soup* book. My sister, Jodi, underwent a very emotional, psychological and spiritual struggle as she dealt with the fact that her long-term boyfriend, Tim, was dying from an inoperable brain tumor. She helped Tim fight his cancer in every way imaginable, but unfortunately on Valentine's Day in 1997, Jodi sat by Tim's side as he took his last breath.

Although her story is tragic, she was able to gain a whole new outlook on the meaning of life and death. She wrote this story about her experience, and it touched me deeply. The power of her words is simply breathtaking, and I wanted to share them with you, and, hopefully, others, as well.

Sincerely,

Kristi Vesterby

Immortal

When someone dies, you don't get over it by forgetting; you get over it by remembering, and you are aware that no person is ever truly lost or gone once they have been in our life and loved us, as we have loved them.

Leslie Marmon Silko

His dizziness and headaches began during the summer; they worried me a little, but I never thought they would amount to anything serious. I look back now and wonder if he knew they were signs of what was to come. Tim and I had been dating for over a year; we'd become best friends. We were in that phase of our lives when we thought nothing could go wrong. We were going to be together forever and live our perfect high-school-sweetheart love story with a white picket fence and all. When his symptoms persisted, I think we both knew that something was wrong, but I never could have imagined just how wrong.

By basketball season, things were considerably worse. It was his junior year, and Tim had hoped he would finally be starting on the varsity team. I would sit in the stands and cheer with the rest of my friends, but inside I was constantly wondering who this impostor was that was taking over Tim's body. He bobbled the ball as he'd dribble up the court, or tip over on the backs of his heels while attempting to play defense. His frustration increased with each day of practice, so when his mother, Ann, suggested he see a doctor, Tim agreed. The local clinic scheduled an appointment for him to have a scan of his brain the next time the "MRI-Mobile" came to Olivia, our small, unequipped town. The scan later showed a tumor growing on the base of Tim's brain, and from then on our lives were never the same.

We all sat crammed in an incredibly small room they called a doctor's office, waiting for the arrival of some overly busy neuro-oncologist. He was going to interpret the complicated X rays that were beyond the capability of the doctors at Prairie Family Practice. This room was as close to hell as I've ever been, and without even knowing what was ahead of me, it was difficult to find a way to pass the time. None of us wanted to think about why we were there, so we mostly occupied the passing minutes with the idle talk of basketball and history class. The oncologist finally graced us with his presence as he walked into our crowded room. He introduced himself and started discussing what we already knew from the scans. Tim had a tumor invading his brain stem. He went on to say that it was inoperable, which meant very little to me at the time. As he went into medical jargon, his words became mere background noise as I turned my attention toward Tim.

He sat in the chair directly across from me, listening to every word the doctor was saying. He was motionless; even his eyes seemed to be staring into a place that had somehow captured his whole being. Tim hated his eyes. He often joked about their "ugly" tint, which he called green-brown-yellow-orangish. I always had to remind him that despite their lack of definite color, his eyes were one of his best features. They disclosed his every emotion. All I had to do was look at them and I could actually see his love for me. His eyes revealed his kindness, his cocky and somewhat rebellious nature, and, of course, his spark of determination. Now they were vacant.

Ann, Tim's mother, asked a question, and I was thrown back into the conversation at hand. Dr. So-and-So answered by discussing the options that could be attempted to shrink the tumor. I wondered why none of his so-called options sounded promising. As this thought meandered through my mind, his mother, with a voice that attempted to hide the quivering, asked how long Tim was expected to live. Her words snuck up from behind me and grabbed my throat. I looked at her as though she was a murderer with no conscience. How could she ask such a question? Tim was not going to die, and she had no right to even suggest that he might. In a detached voice void of all emotion the doctor said, "One year to eighteen months with treatment."

As he spoke these words, the grip around my neck tightened to the point of choking me. I struggled for a breath, and the already tiny room closed even more. I needed space, and the first thought that crossed my mind was to run, not only from the room, but from the whole situation. I could escape now before I got hurt. I was confused and angry, but most of all I was consumed by the incredible fear of losing someone I loved so much.

I looked at Tim who sat motionless; he didn't say anything and neither did anyone else. The room was filled with an uncomfortable silence, and I could feel the pulse of my heart pounding in my ears. I was sure that everyone could hear me sucking in each breath. I don't remember what the doctor said before he left the room—I couldn't even look at this man who had just sentenced Tim to death. When we were alone, Ann crossed the room and gave Tim a hug. The rest of us sat and cried. Tim looked up and with a smile said, "I'm not going anywhere." It was his declaration of war.

I was nervous, and I didn't know what I should do. I was just the girlfriend; I didn't know if I had any business being a part of this ordeal. As I was thinking that this was a time their family should be alone, Ann left Tim's side and he motioned for me to come over. I sat down on his knee and, wrapping my arms around his neck, rested my forehead against his. When I opened my eyes they met his, and I saw the emotion in them that had been missing up to that point. Water welled up on the brim of his lids, and finally a single tear fell, gliding down his cheek in slow motion.

Tim had always had the fighter attitude, and I believed him completely when he said he was going to beat the odds that were stacked against him. The battle was on. He was going to do everything he could in order to conquer the cancer threatening to overtake the life that he wasn't done living. His life became a quest to find a physical cure. He viewed it as a challenge he needed to overcome, and there was no doubt in his mind that he would do it.

His battle was viewed as courageous; he became a local hero. Why is it that people with terminal illness are so respected for fighting for a cure until the end? Do they even have a choice? The focus always lies in finding a physical remedy. Do everything and anything you can to battle the disease. What have you got to lose? Don't give up. Rarely do you find people looking for a type of healing that restores the soul. I guess that's just not good enough. Death meant failure, and that was unacceptable. So along with everything else, I encouraged Tim to stay strong and fight. I wanted him to do whatever he could to beat the cancer. I didn't realize that it didn't have to be a war. Nobody had to be the loser. I wish I would have known that then.

He was bombarded by alternative healing options, some more "far out" than others, but all promising a miraculous cure. There was no way he could try all of them. Tim choked down over seventy pills a day: shark cartilage, herbal remedies, beta this and turbo that, each one offering a way to fight his growing tumor. He forced himself to drink glass after glass of carrot juice despite the thick texture, pungent odor and lingering aftertaste. He tried some positive-imagery techniques and then there was that magnetic contraption. The list goes on.

The traditional medical world was also involved in the battle, despite their lack of confidence in a cure. Surgery was out of the question because of the tumor's location, so the doctors suggested other treatment options. The Duke University brain-tumor team provided a protocol that involved heavy doses of radiation therapy, shooting directly at the base of his brain stem two times a day for several months. The tumor shrunk by half, but it wasn't annihilated; in fact, it was fighting back. Eventually chemotherapy, a word that had quickly became as taboo as profanity in church, was attempted as a last resort. It didn't work.

I was included in Tim's battle against cancer in

almost every way possible, and the Orth family always made me feel welcome. I went where Tim went. I don't know if his parents always approved (or mine for that matter), but as long as it kept Tim happy, they didn't complain. I went along on all the hospital visits. I went on family trips. I spent more time at their house than I should admit, but it was worth it. I rapidly evolved from my "just a girlfriend" status to member of their clan. I loved them, and still do.

Tim's health declined rapidly during the last months of his life. His former physique was reduced to a loose layer of skin covering his skeleton. It was difficult to keep him comfortable, and he spent most of his days hunched on the reclining sofa in his living room. I spent most of my days in the seat beside him watching him sleep. Sometimes the selfishness in me would overpower my good sense, and I would wake him from a peaceful sleep so that I could talk to him.

In a matter of months I watched my boyfriend turn into an eighty-year-old man. He went blind, he couldn't walk, he couldn't remember, but he could still laugh. I experienced a crash course in Nursing 101, quickly learning all of the details involved in caring for someone who is terminally ill. However, I soon realized that my most important "job responsibility" was to keep a smile on Tim's face. It's difficult to maintain dignity when you can't do anything for yourself. He had to cope with issues of aging as a teenager. He was nineteen years old and had to deal with the fact that his girlfriend had to help him go to the bathroom. I cracked jokes and teased him about silly things to lighten his mood. I basically treated him like I always had; I was the person who didn't minister to him like he was dying. I made him laugh. It was the only thing I could do to help in a seemingly helpless situation, but it wasn't enough. I wanted to help him be at peace, even though I wasn't. One day after waking up from a regular afternoon nap, I noticed that Tim's eyes were focused in a dreamlike manner on something in the upper-right corner of the living room. He was mesmerized by what he was seeing, and the slight grin across his face suggested it was something awesome. It took me a few seconds to remember that Tim was blind because the tumor was slowly overtaking the optic nerve's space in his brain. I wondered what he could be looking at.

"Tim, what are you staring at?" I asked, though I wasn't sure I was ready to hear his answer.

"Just the light up there," he replied, continuing to stare ahead. The tears raced to my eyes, but I blinked to keep them from falling. I knew in my heart what he was seeing, but I wasn't satisfied with his vague answer. I wanted more.

"I can't see it. What is it like?" I asked.

"It's beautiful. You're not supposed to see it, though."

"Tell me about it," I probed with a combination of curiosity and fear. Tim didn't take his eyes off the spot in the corner of the room. He had several false starts before he was finally able to form the words he was searching for.

"I'm going up there . . . soon." The tears that had been welling in my eyes up to that point were released like floodgates. For the first time, I was grateful for Tim's blindness; I didn't want him to see me cry. I cleared my throat, in an attempt to get rid of the lump that had formed there, and took a deep breath, letting it out slowly to help me relax. This might be my last opportunity to talk to Tim about facing death, and I wasn't going to allow my emotions to let it slip away. I had so much I needed to tell him, for my own sake and for his. I wanted Tim to experience a peaceful death, and I did not want to be the one who was holding him back. I told him he could leave whenever he was ready. I explained that I would be okay after he left.

"I love you so much," I said, "and I am going to miss you more than you could possibly imagine. It will be so hard to live the rest of my life without you here, but I know that one day I'll see you again." Tim's attention was finally diverted from the heavenly focus. He reached over and held his hand out for me to hold. A smirk took over the peaceful expression that had been occupying his face and he let out a weak chuckle.

"That part is up to you," he said, completely amused with his insinuation that I had better be good while he was gone if I wanted to join him in eternity. He could never pass up a good smart remark. I laughed and cried. I felt a sense of relief. There was no way I could have said everything that needed to be said, and of course, everything didn't come out the way I intended it to. However, Tim and I were able to share an experience that offered us both a sense of closure. It was the closest to heaven that I have been in my lifetime, and I'll never forget it.

I left Tim's house on February 13 feeling disheartened. I always got a kiss from Tim before leaving; it was a custom I'd grown used to. He would sit with his eyes closed and his lips puckered, waiting for me to bend down and say good night. Tonight things were different. Tim had slipped into a comalike state and was still incoherent as I prepared to leave. I bent down to kiss him good-bye, and his labored breathing was magnified. My lips touched his, and all hope for a response was lost. As I put on my coat and boots, I remembered that the next day was Valentine's Day. I had told him earlier that the best gift he could give me was for him to be at peace. As I closed the front door behind me, I wondered if he heard.

With a bunch of red and white balloons in hand, I entered the Orths' house the next morning. I knew he wouldn't be able to see the gift I'd brought, but I needed to bring something. Tim was lying lifeless in his high-tech hospice bed, but I could see his chest moving as he took each breath, and was relieved that he hadn't gone without me by his side. I spent the morning curled up next to him in his bed, holding his hand. Around 12:30, Tim took his last breaths. I don't recall the exact moment he died; I only remember opening my eyes and he was gone. His mother proclaimed, "Oh, Tim, no more seizures, no more headaches. Now you can see. Now you can laugh. Now you can run. Now you can fly! We love you!"

I didn't have any profound words; I'm not good with good-byes. I whispered, "See ya later."

Although Tim's life on earth ended on February 14, 1997, he continues to live on in so many other ways. Tim helped me to be the person that I am today. He taught me that the most important part of living is to find happiness in everything. I look back on all the memorable moments we shared together, and I recall his immortality. I remember all the fishless fishing trips. I remember eating popcorn and playing endless games of cribbage at my kitchen table. I remember cringing every time a song by Prince came on the radio because I knew he would sing along. I remember keeping my parents up all night with our outbursts of laughter, and I remember falling asleep on the couch listening to his heartbeat.

I know I will experience love again, but I will never find a replacement for what I had. Instead, I will take Tim with me as I continue to live my life. He will be with me when I graduate from college. He will be with me when my father walks me down the aisle at my wedding. He will be with me when I teach my first child to throw a softball. Eventually we will be together again when it's my time to leave this Earth.

Jodi Vesterby

Unconditional Love

Dear Chicken Soup for the Teenage Soul,

Ever since I can remember, my father has had a problem with alcohol. When I was little, he and my mother would have fights. My mother, sister and I would have to pack up our bags and stay with my grandmother. We must have done that ten times, but I was so young and naïve then. I never paid much attention to the fact that every drink my father consumed affected how long he would actually live.

About two years ago, my father was officially diagnosed with alcoholism, a disease that controls your thoughts and emotions to the point where you cannot function without alcohol. I never saw my father as anyone with problems. He was my undying superhero, capable of overcoming every obstacle in his way. In his high-school years, he was labeled "The American Dream." He was a high-school track star, handsome and talented. Unfortunately, my father grew up with an alcoholic father much like himself. I wish he hadn't inherited his father's tendencies.

Recently my father was in an alcohol-related accident, a head-on collision with another car. It was this accident that made me realize how serious his illness really was. I clearly remember the phone call we received that night, at 2:00 A.M. I picked up the phone and was asked to put on the lady of the house. I hurriedly awoke my mother and gave her the phone. I watched as she listened to the grueling details. *What if he doesn't make it?* I thought as I sobbed. She hung up the phone and told me not to cry, that everything would be okay. I watched from the window through tears as she pulled out of our driveway to go to the hospital. I stayed up all night by the phone, waiting to hear that my father was going to be okay.

Finally at seven in the morning, the phone rang. He had been under the influence and without a seat belt. His head had smashed through the windshield, cutting open his face and damaging his brain. He had been unconscious when they pulled him from the car, and his eye was completely exposed. My mom had seen him before they took him to surgery, and she said that she thought he was dead. He looked horrible. Luckily, the doctors, with the help of God, were able to save my father and prevent permanent damage to his right eye.

Now the doctors are telling us that my father will die if he doesn't quit drinking. He's only forty-five years old. Even if he does quit drinking they will eventually have to transplant his severely damaged liver.

My dad, the once-beautiful track star, has changed. His hair has thinned, and his skin is scarred. His legs are black from lack of blood circulation; his once sky-blue eyes are no longer bright, but lackluster; and the whites of his eyes are yellow.

If you ask me, though, my daddy is still beautiful and he's still my hero, my American Dream. But one with a life-threatening disease.

There has never been a greater pain than witnessing my father, someone I love and look up to more than anyone in the world, slowly killing himself. And I pray every day that God will help free my father of his alcoholism.

If you're reading this, Dad, I want you to know that I love you. I am proud of you and all the things that you have accomplished. You are still my hero and my superdad. You have strength in you, Daddy, to overcome drinking. I know you do. Everyone makes mistakes, and God offers many chances. Daddy-O, this is your chance; please come back to us.

I am writing this letter in hopes that anyone with this disease in their family will know that they are not alone. With the love and support of family members and friends, this disease is conquerable.

Thanks,

Rachel Palmer

Guy Repellent

Dear Chicken Soup for the Teenage Soul,

I have always enjoyed the *Chicken Soup for the Teenage Soul* books, however I haven't really been able to relate to any of the stories in the Relationships chapter. You see, I have never been in a relationship before so I am not able to feel the emotions of the authors. The stories are either about people in relationships or having just come out of one. There don't seem to be any stories addressing the insecurities and sad feelings people have who have never been in a relationship and feel weird because of it.

I have always believed that I was born with a coating of guy repellent. Like bug repellent, it drives away guys instead of bugs. To me, relation-ships have always required time, patience and the big "L" word, love. The idea of being in a relation-ship has always made me sort of squeamish and reluctant. Kissing scenes on TV would bring me to close my eyes. Couples on the street, in the malls or any other public place showing affection towards each other annoyed me. Couldn't they do it elsewhere? Some people told me that I was going through a phase and things would soon change. They were sort of right. I developed my first crush, and secretly spent time thinking about that person. I had begun to accept the fact that people falling in love is part of our everyday lives.

When I began high school it suddenly hit me that everyone had grown up, while I was still a child. Everyone seemed like they were experts on dating, since many had practically started at age four. They knew everything and could give advice as if they were trained professionals. I, on the other hand, had never gone out with a single person, nor had anyone shown the slightest bit of interest in me. Even though I wasn't interested in anyone either, it made me feel bad, and the more I thought about it, the worse I felt. Was I ugly? What was wrong with me?

I knew that I wasn't the most attractive person or the most popular, but I certainly wasn't ugly. I would observe girls who had dated an endless string of guys and wonder what it was about them that made the guys go crazy. Some of them were very ordinary, and not even pretty. Others acted like ditzes.

One day while talking to a girl in my music class, the topic of relationships came up. I mentioned to her how I always managed to end up empty-handed in the dating pool. I remember her saying, "There's nothing wrong with that. Besides, the only two boyfriends I have ever had, I had to ask out." Her response startled me. She was one of those girls who seemed to attract tons of guys. She was gorgeous, with thick hair, beautiful brown eyes with green flecks, and a great personality to match. I started feeling better about my relationship predicament. I realized there was really nothing wrong with me if even people like her had to work to make relationships happen.

Since that day, I've finally discovered that I have to accept myself for who I am, both my strengths and my weaknesses. I have a tendency to look serious most of the time, which makes me appear unfriendly and cold, even though that is not what I am. Yes, I focus on school and hang out in the library, but I've learned never to sacrifice the things that I believe in just to impress a guy. After all, you can only pretend for so long. Whoever I end up with will have to like me for who I am, the nice girl who, according to her classmates, is destined to become a future nun. I feel that's the way a relationship should be. Until I meet that special person, I will be busy enjoying who I am and all the things I love doing. Who knows, maybe I *will* become a nun. My future is not really clear to me now. I'll just have to wait and see. Guy repellent or not, I'm going to be just fine.

Thanks,

Erin Seto

Always a Tomorrow

Dear Chicken Soup for the Teenage Soul,

My name is Ashley, and I am fourteen years old. I am writing to share a page I completed in my *Chicken Soup for the Teenage Soul Journal*. The journal asked us to write what we would say to someone who was suicidal. The exercise was very good for me. It was a release. I guess I had been holding a lot of feelings inside and needed a place to express them. So many kids my age talk about suicide. It's everywhere—I hear about it at school, on TV, in the movies and in magazines. It's the ultimate escape. It even seems like teens glamorize it these days. I remember first understanding the concept of somebody trying to take his or her life when I was ten years old. It shocked me then and it shocks me now.

I have my bad days just like everyone else. I have days when I feel like I just can't take it anymore or just can't go on. But fortunately I have always seemed to find the strength within myself to pick up the pieces and move on. There is always a tomorrow. When I completed this page in my journal, it made me realize how strongly I feel about being able to reach out to all those who feel suicidal. That's when I got the idea to send the page to you. I hope that somebody, somewhere will get the message that suicide is not the answer.

Your books have helped me realize that I am not alone in my suffering and that the teen years are difficult for many. Thank you for giving us outlets like the journal to express our feelings and learn about ourselves.

Sincerely,

Ashley Lusk

My Letter

HEY YOU!

Yeah, you. The one with the pill bottle or loaded pistol in your hand. Can you stop for a second and think about what you're doing? That bullet <u>will</u> create a hole in your head and that rope <u>will</u> turn your face a cold gray.

So what's the problem? Too much work? Parents a pain? Did you get dumped? Is it really worth losing a great future over, whatever it may be? Right now you may think so, but ten years down the road, when you hold your first child in your arms, will you feel the same? I'm not going to sugarcoat it. Your parents may be total jerks and you might be under too much pressure, but is it really worth finding out what happens when you die? If you still want to swallow those pills or drink that bleach, it doesn't seem like you're thinking this through enough.

I've been where you are. Life is like a game show. Sometimes you get a big boat, and sometimes you only get some crummy car wax. All you can do is spin the wheel again and hope for a better prize. And you can't say someone doesn't love you, because everyone has someone who loves them. I love you. I love you with all the love a teenager can have.

So, drop that murderer in your hand, whatever it is, and know you will be okay. Things always are.

Love,

Somebody who cares

April 15, the Worst and Best Day of My Life

I'm just glad that now this rainstorm has ended, and I can see the rainbow once again.

Rebecca Spanier

Dear Chicken Soup for the Teenage Soul,

April 15 was the worst day of my life. I was nineteen years old. My body felt achy, my mind was cloudy and I felt as if I couldn't go on any longer. My face was pale, and my nerves were frazzled. It was on that day that I faced the biggest decision I have ever made.

Although I had dealt with depression before, it wasn't until the last few years when it really hit hard. It had become so bad that most days it was all I could do to keep breathing. On the outside I looked like a smart, happy and talented teenager. On the inside I was wilted and dying.

Things just kept on getting worse. I got to the point to where I truly hated myself. I started to become self-destructive and ended up in therapy. My therapist tried to help me, and although I attended my weekly session and took my medication, it didn't help. I started to binge and purge and lost thirty pounds. I started to cut myself, using knives and sharp items to make me bleed. Because I couldn't understand or handle the emotional pain, I preferred the physical pain because I knew where it came from. My days were filled with thoughts of how I'd end my life and what I'd write in my suicide note. I also began to hurt my family and friends, pushing them away and saying hurtful things to them. I wanted them to hate me as much as I hated myself. They were only trying to help, but I couldn't, wouldn't accept help from anyone; not from my therapist, my friends or my family. I was too afraid to open up. I let all my emotions and feelings stay bottled up inside me. I had hit bottom—I was broken down and couldn't go any further into my hole. I didn't know what else to do.

So on April 15, after a sleepless night, I had to make a decision that would affect the rest of my life. As I saw it, I had two choices—to give up and give in, or to fight.

After showering and trying to make my body look human, I got into my car and drove. I cried, and my mind was spinning. I felt like I was going to pass out, but I had made my choice and I promised myself I'd follow through no matter what. I finally arrived at my therapist's office, and spilled out the whole story: the cutting, the suicidal thoughts, everything. I felt as if my self-constructed dam of emotions had burst. Old pent-up emotions and feelings came rushing out and wouldn't stop. It came as a surprise to both of us—I hadn't talked much in therapy. It had been so hard to allow myself to be vulnerable with someone, and now I was letting her in on my darkest pain. And it was such a relief.

I drove home exhausted. I knew I had to tell my parents everything that was going on and I knew how hard it was going to be. It would hurt them to hear, just as much as it would hurt me to tell the truth. They were wonderful. That day and for days after, my large, extended family and friends sur-rounded me with love and support. They let me know how much I mattered to them—and for the first time in my life, I felt true love and happiness. Being honest about my feelings wasn't nearly as painful as I thought it would be; it actually felt incredible to finally express myself openly.

It's been a long road. Even now, I still get down and have hard days, but it's different. The darkness doesn't last as long and the depression isn't as bad. I'm twenty now and in my second year of college. I work part-time, sing in a choir and teach drama to junior-high kids. I can finally let people love me and allow myself to love them back. I'm looking forward to becoming all that I can be. April 15 was the best day of my life, and I'll always remember it.

Thank you so much for your books. I hope my story will be one that helps others as much as certain stories have helped me.

Sincerely,

Laurel Walker

Hope

Dear Chicken Soup for the Teenage Soul,

After my story "Losing Hope"* was published in *Chicken Soup for the Teenage Soul II*, I received quite a number of letters and phone calls, most of them from teenagers who were touched by my story. This was very gratifying—knowing that my story touched these people in some important way.

I am enclosing one of the letters that affected me the most. In *Teen II*, my story starts with Carrie reading a line from a poem she had composed in seventh grade, "Hope is the hat rack upon which I hang my dreams. . . ." A number of readers decided to finish the poem and send it to me. Needless to say, this touched me deeply. The

---

* *"Losing Hope," by Heather Klassen,* Chicken Soup for the Teenage Soul II, *pp. 116–120.*

following poem is one I would like to, in turn, share with you. Thank you for the opportunity to share in the work you are doing.

Sincerely,
Heather Klassen

From "Losing Hope":

"Hope is the hat rack upon which I hang my dreams . . ."? Oh, please! I crumple up the paper and fling it across my bedroom. I can't believe I kept my hopeless seventh-grade attempts at poetry. I thought I was a poet that year. Obviously I wasn't, and never will be.

"Here they are," I mutter, pulling a stack of year-books from the depths of the drawer. They go all the way back to elementary school. Lauren will like these. Best friends since first grade, she's not talking to me now, but I'm sure she'll want these . . . after . . .

Dear Heather,

My name is Kelsey Brunone. I am thirteen years old and live in Harleysville, Pennsylvania. I have an older sister, who is fifteen, and two pets. I enjoy writing, reading, talking on the phone (or anywhere, really) and I like going on my computer. I am writing to you about a story you wrote in <u>Chicken Soup for the Teenage Soul II</u>. I have read almost all of the <u>Chicken Soup for the Soul</u> books, including both teenage volumes. The story you contributed, titled "Losing Hope," really affected me.

The emotions and feelings you described in your piece totally related to my life. The feelings of frustration and sadness and of not being able to find a niche in life connected with me so well that I was in tears at the end of the story. It is one that I have gone back and read many times when I was feeling lost or lonely. Although I have never attempted suicide the way the character has, I know how it feels to think that is the only way out of your problem. All my life I have wanted to be a writer, someone who can put the strongest of emotions down on paper and help the reader to feel what you are feeling. You have accomplished that.

Like a friend whenever you need her, this story has meant more than words on a page. It helped me to understand and see so much more clearly. I am not sure if you ever completed the poem, "Hope is the hat rack upon which I hang my dreams. . . ." I am sending you my completion of the poem. Please keep this as a thank-you gift from me to you for writing this inspirational story.

Thank you again for helping me through these adolescent years and for taking the time to let you what a wonderful writer you are.

Sincerely,

Kelsey Brunone

Hope

Hope is the rack
Which I hang my dreams upon
Carefully placing
One article of my future on
Hope.

Hope is the box
Which I place my thoughts in
Gingerly folding
My aspirations into
Trying.

Hope is the shelf
Which I sit my fears on
Cautiously tucking
Them away from
Striving.

Hope is the rack
Which I hang my success on
Proudly displaying
All I have accomplished with the help of
Hope.

Kelsey Brunone

Am I Helping . . . ?

Dear Chicken Soup,

As a writer, I've often asked myself, *Am I helping to change the world with my words? Am I making a difference in anyone's life?*

Dear Cheryl,

I read your poem "Making Sarah Cry," in <u>Chicken Soup for the Teenage Soul II.</u> I have to thank you; it made me realize how much I love my little sister. You see, this poem reminds me of her. She, too, is named Sarah, and this is the same kind of torture she endures every day of her life, even when she's not at school. I'm not proud to say that it is my fault. I tease her and ignore her relentlessly, and I have noticed she still loves me. I have decided I need to apologize and change my ways and thank her for loving me when I did not deserve it.

Sincerely,
Amanda

The character Sarah from my poem, "Making Sarah Cry"* has made many lessons real for me. I have received letters from those who were bullies and sadly, those who are bullied. I have cried over those letters; tears of happiness and tears of sadness, and have learned many valuable lessons as well. It's never too late to change, and it's wonderful to offer words of kindness to someone. After all, you just might make someone's day that ordinarily might have been a miserable one, just as so many giving teens have often "made my day" with their letters.

You see, there have been times when I've felt like putting my pen and paper away for good. Not because I don't love to write, but because I often feel as if the only thing I'm accomplishing by writing is a broken heart. After all, writers want to be published; they want their words to mean something to someone. It's hard to be rejected by publishers, and more often than not my work is

---

*"Making Sarah Cry," by Cheryl L. Costello-Forshey, Chicken Soup for the Teenage Soul II, pp. 214–217.

rejected rather than accepted, so the letters I have received not only brought a much-needed smile to my face, they gave me the "acceptance" I needed as a writer to continue writing. Thanks to those wonderful, courageous teens who have written to me, I now know I am making a difference in someone's life.

Dear Cheryl,

After reading your poem, I began to realize how many times I had joined my friends in ridiculing fellow classmates simply to show how cool I was. I decided that wasn't who I was, or how I wanted people to see me. Two days after this realization, I was chosen to be a captain for a basketball tournament in my gym class. I chose a girl who everyone picked on. My next choice was a girl who had never played sports in her life. I warily but determinedly made two more similar selections for my team. My gym teacher pulled me aside after the teams were picked and asked me why I had chosen the way I had. I simply explained that none of the girls had ever been picked any better than last. I didn't care if we won a single game, or even scored a single basket. I just wanted them to know that they were a part of something that really mattered to me.

Thank you for making a positive change in my heart. As for pursuing a career in writing, I can only hope that I will someday write something as inspirational as "Making Sarah Cry."

Sincerely,

Melissa

Dear Melissa,

You already have, Melissa; you already have. . . .

Sincerely,

Cheryl L. Costello-Forshey
author, "Making Sarah Cry"

Sharing an Intimate Moment

Dear Chicken Soup,

I have lived in Southern California my whole life. I was never part of the popular crowd in high school. I never had the best grades or kept up on my who-is-dating-who gossip. The only things that interested me were hanging out with my friends and being on time for my horseback riding lessons. I didn't set foot in an airport until I was sixteen and had my first boyfriend when I was seventeen.

I have never had much luck with guys. I don't like the idea of breaking up over something dumb and crying for a week about how much he hurt me, so I usually end things early. Just before my eighteenth birthday, I met the most beautiful guy. He was really sweet to me so I thought maybe he would be different from other guys. I really let myself like him; I trusted him.

On my eighteenth birthday, I went to school because I had two tests to take, one of which I failed. My friends had brought me balloons, but the wind took the biggest and prettiest one. Then the rain began to pour down on me. My birthday was not going very well, and worst of all, when I went to my boyfriend's house he broke up with me!

For the next day, I stayed in my room until my mom offered to take me to lunch. She presented me with *Chicken Soup for the Teenage Soul*. Reading the stories made me feel so much better. Even though I didn't know the people who wrote the stories, I felt connected to them. They made me feel good inside.

I have written about something that happened to me at summer camp that I would like to share with others in hopes that they too can get something positive from it. I hope it makes at least someone feel better, like others have done for me.

Sincerely,

Emily Ferry

Camp Confidence

"Mike! Camp question," Reese declared. "Now, the camp question, for those of you who don't know, is: Out of all the counselors at Meadow Oaks summer camp who would you get together with?"

Mike sat for a second contemplating his decision. "Well, I could take the easy way out and say Monica," he grinned, "but I am not going to do that." He paused again before saying, "I would have to say the horse girl, Emily."

Okay, this is where I have to back up a bit. See, my name happens to be Emily. The conversation taking place above happened at a Meadow Oaks summer camp campout. It was two weeks before the end of camp, and my friend Reese and I had decided to attend the campout. When the kids were all asleep, the counselors made their way to the arts and crafts building where we all sat in a big circle and played Truth or Dare . . . without the dare. The people in the circle ranged in age from sixteen to their early twenties. This game made me feel as if I was back in high school, but it was fun to find out what people thought about everyone else at camp.

Since Reese and I worked in the area of horses we didn't see or hear much of what went on with the other counselors. Mike certainly never came down to see us. We attended camp parties and staff events and had gotten to know a lot of the counselors, but we were still pretty much out of the loop. I had had a crush on Mike all summer, but he was a part of the really popular clique and I deemed him untouchable since he could pretty much have anyone he wanted. But during the last week of camp he paid more attention to me than before. Reese insisted he liked me, but I paid it no mind. Well, the campout certainly changed my view. This is where I return to the previous conversation.

". . . the horse girl, Emily," Mike said.

I sat in the darkness not sure what to think. Mike had just picked me out of all the other girls at camp. I sat for a minute while Reese chimed in my ear with, "I told you so." A few minutes later, Mike stood up and told me to follow him. I asked where we were going, and he said to follow. I heard the quiet oohs from the people in the circle as I stood and followed him to the back of the arts and crafts building.

He stood in front of me for a minute and turned his toe in, smiling like a little boy. "I can't believe I told all those people I like you," he said. I smiled at the sight of his twenty-three-year-old shyness, but when I began to say something back he pulled me close and kissed me sweetly. Now, at nineteen I had received my share of kisses, but something about Mike's kiss was different. It seemed more sincere than any I had gotten in the past. I felt as if I would float away.

Mike left for a teaching job in San Diego two days later. I have seen him a few times, but nothing ever came of our night at the campout. Circumstance wouldn't allow for it. But ever since that night I have walked with my head a little higher and looked in the mirror at a face I finally see as pretty . . . all because I was picked by one seemingly unattainable boy.

Emily Ferry

Treasuring a Friend

And after all the heartbreaks, and the fights, and the tears, and the anger, true love will be waiting for you at the end . . . and it will be worth it.

Elizabeth Fischer

Dear Chicken Soup for the Teenage Soul,

I have to say I enjoy your books *so* much. I never thought the contents could have such an enormous impact on a reader's life as they have had on mine. Your books, along with some other events in my life, have helped me realize what an amazing person my boyfriend, David, really is and that I should treasure him.

Just the other day, David gave me a vase of purple flowers and a stress ball, because I have been agonizing over college applications and stressing during my senior year. He's done countless special things like this for me over the last year and a half that we've been together.

I met David for the first time during my freshman year. He was a sophomore, and we had a world history class together. We made a few feeble attempts to speak to each other, but nothing more than just a few friendly words were exchanged—no real conversation to speak of. I found out later, though, that on the last day of school that year he was going to ask me for my phone number, but right when he decided to do it the bell rang and I was gone.

That summer came and went, but during my sophomore year I met up with him through my friend, Mark, and my best friend, Jon. The four of us hung out together almost every day. By the middle of June, David asked me out and we became a couple.

One of the things that puts David on a higher pedestal than the other guys I have dated is his incredible sweetness toward my sister, Christine. She has Down's syndrome, a mentally debilitating disorder that causes her mental processes to be slower than the average person's. She is an extremely lovable girl, and we're very close.

The very first day David met Christine, he treated

her with total respect. He never talked to her like she was a child, but instead he looked at her as though she was just like him or me. The three of us would go out sometimes to the movies or bowling.

When my junior year began, we started fighting a lot, and our relationship began to deteriorate. As Homecoming approached, we were fighting more and more. We broke up, and I ended up going out with Mark. Instead of David trying to get back at me, he asked Christine to go with him to the dance. She had never been to a high-school dance and for David to ask her to go with him was so exciting. At first I was a little confused and somewhat surprised why David had asked my sister and not some other girl.

The day of the dance came quickly. David and I had earlier reached a truce so that we could all go in a group and have a good time with each other. I helped Christine pick out her dress, and we did our hair together. She was so excited and nervous that I had to calm her down at least once an hour. She called all of her friends to remind them that she was going to Homecoming.

When David and Mark came to pick us up it was raining. Christine opened the door and David was standing on the porch with a huge corsage in one hand and a black umbrella in the other. He came in, put on her corsage and smiled for pictures with her. Mark and I did the same, and then we were off. David took Christine's arm and escorted her to the car and opened and closed the door for her. At the restaurant, he pulled out her chair and read her the menu. She had a huge smile on her face the entire night. When the night was over, he kissed her on the cheek and told her that he had one of the best nights of his life.

After watching David and Christine at Homecoming, it finally sunk in how special he really was. Very few guys would do something as sweet as David had done. Maybe to him it was just a simple thing, but it meant the world to Christine. For one night she was just like every other high-school girl at a dance. Nobody singled her out or even so much as smirked at her. It boosted her low self-esteem. I don't think David realized what an impact he had on my sister that evening, but I am happily reminded of it whenever I go in her room and see their Homecoming picture hanging on her wall.

David and I got back together again shortly after Homecoming, and we are a very happy couple to this day. (In fact, I should end this letter here because the flowers he gave me need some water, and I want them to last!)

Best wishes,

Laura Motyka

My Dad, My Source for Healing

Dear Editors of Chicken Soup,

I have been gobbling up your stories for years. I own all your books (and the game, too). I love what each story has to offer in its meaning and new perspective on life. I would like to take the opportunity to share what got me through a difficult breakup in high school—my dad.

When most of my friends were bickering with their fathers, I was looking to mine for guidance. He knows more about me than anyone, even myself at times. He travels for work and so he's gone a lot. Most people assume we have a distant relationship because he's not home very often. But we thrive under this situation because we talk every night by phone, and he makes his support known when he can't be present. One night my world just collapsed, and it was my dad who was able to pick up the pieces.

My first true love called from a party and broke my heart. He offered little explanation and this made the situation all the more difficult to accept. In that one quick phone call I lost my boyfriend and best friend, a comfort I had enjoyed for the past year and a half. I was sure I was the most miserable fifteen-year-old in the world—lost and lonely. It felt like everyone else's life could just continue on in its normal way, but mine couldn't. I would no longer spend hours on the phone with him each night, and his house would no longer be my home away from home.

I was forced to deal with my regular routine on Monday morning, as Mom went to work, Dad flew out on business and I went to school. Dad wouldn't return until Friday. I wasn't sure how I was going to be able to face everyone and their gossip at school. I was right: the questions and the whispering started around second period.

I returned home from school feeling completely defeated. All I wanted to do was crawl into bed and wallow in my own self-pity. I pulled back the covers on my bed and discovered a pile of cards left by my dad. I recognized the "calligraphy" instantly. Each card included an instruction that it was to be opened on a particular night that week. He was halfway across the country and still my dad was able to show he cared.

I made it through that week because of him. Each card seemed to say just what I needed to hear. Tuesday's card said, "The past is painful to think about and the future is impossible to envision. Don't try. Just take it one minute at a time." On Wednesday my mood lifted when I read, "What you are feeling now is natural and normal. It still feels lousy, but it is part of the healing process." Friday's card contained a poem he wrote. The last lines made me smile through my tears. "Whatever special challenges you face along life's way/May you trust that you will find the best in every day." I was instructed to open the last card after the party I went to on Saturday night. In it he sagely reminded me to laugh. "The world isn't so bad after a good laugh. The more you laugh, the more you heal." Each card was signed, *Love, Dad*.

Even just flipping through the cards made me feel better in the weeks to come. I looked through them most days until I started to forget about them. It was then that I knew that I was healing.

Sincerely,

Kelsey Cameron

A Simple Smile, a Scream Inside

Dear Chicken Soup for the Teenage Soul,

My name is Stephanie. I am sixteen years old. I started writing after my mom was admitted to the hospital for depression. I soon became depressed myself. Writing became my means of expressing myself through those difficult times. No matter how painful or sad the world around me was, when I had a piece of paper and a pen, I could make the whole world brighter. The words seemed to dance, flowing from pen to paper flooding my world with sunshine the way light floods a dark room when the door is opened. What really kept me going was the vague sense of a goal that I wanted to reach, the hope that one day someone else could read my poems and get something out of them.

I have learned so much about myself from

reading your book. I only hope that when others read my poetry they can have the same experience: to learn something about themselves or feel a moment of happiness. That's what dreams are all about. Hopefully, someday mine will come true.

Thank you,
Stephanie Schultz

A Simple Smile, a Scream Inside

There's so much no one knows,
So much that no one sees,
About the way I feel inside, my thoughts and all my needs.

Maybe it's that they don't look,
Or the fact that I don't show,
Either way, there are things inside that no one seems to know.

I want to show the world.
I want everyone to see.
All the thoughts and the ideas that flow inside of me.

Maybe you haven't noticed,
Or maybe you don't dare,
To find out who I am, to show me that you care.

I'm screaming on the inside,

A smile is what you see,

But I am not content with the person I seem to be.

There's a different person on the inside,

That I can't seem to show,

But maybe if you took the time, that person you could know.

Stephanie Schultz

Whatever I Want to Be

Dear Chicken Soup,

My name is Renee Tanner. I am fifteen years old and an interracial child. My father is black, and my mother is white. I do not consider myself either black or white. I won't even say that I am mixed. I like to define myself as me, for skin color is really of little importance. It is part of the exterior, not the interior. I believe that what matters most is what's inside your heart, not what color skin you have. However, I have not always felt this way.

From the age of six, I did what every kid did. I went to school and learned, came home, played and just had fun. But there was something inside me that was never quite right. I never felt complete. I felt different in a way. It didn't really affect me until I was older. As time passed, it became harder and harder to just be me.

All through elementary school my best friends were white. The kids at my school seemed as if they did not know that I was both black and white. But once I got into seventh grade I realized that I was different because some of the black kids at my school started to make fun of me, I think because I wasn't entirely black. Also, some of the white kids from the other elementary schools looked at me in a weird sort of way. I was an outcast to them. My best friends never knew how upset I was, because I couldn't tell them. I knew they wouldn't understand. One day I was crying hysterically, and I called a friend of mine. I told her that I didn't fit in. That nobody understood me. And nobody would ever understand me. I said that I was different and that it was impossible for me to just be me. She asked me where I had come up with all of this. I told her that my mother was white and my father was black and I didn't know what I was. Was I mixed? Was I black? Was I white? I didn't know. She said to me, "Renee, you are Renee Elizabeth Tanner. That is who you are. You are everything and anything you want to be." I didn't believe her, but she kept trying to tell me that it didn't matter what I looked like. However, it didn't work, and I continued to believe that I was different.

I couldn't talk to the black people at school, for I

was not fully black, and I couldn't talk to the white people because I was not fully white. It hurt inside to not know who I was, to not be able to fit into a perfect category. For almost a year I cried every night. I wrote poems and stories. I kept everything either inside or on paper. Never once did my friends know how much pain I was in. And some of them still don't know.

One day after crying for hours, I picked up the book my mother had given to me for my birthday, *Chicken Soup for the Teenage Soul.* I began to read it, hoping that it would lift my spirits. Not even ten minutes into the book, I stopped crying. By the time I had finished, I felt something incredible. I felt a sense of belonging. I called my friend again and told her that I no longer felt so alone. Again she said, "Renee, you are whatever you want to be." Finally it hit me.

After all those years of feeling different, I finally came to terms with who I am. My name is Renee Tanner. My parents are black and white. And I, well, I am both of them. I no longer care what color my skin is, or whether black or white people talk to me. The people who are my friends don't care what I look like.

Sincerely,

Renee Tanner

A Loving Change

Dear Chicken Soup for the Teenage Soul,

Yesterday I went out and bought the *Chicken Soup for the Teenage Soul Journal*. I knew the moment I held it in my hand and glanced at a few of the topics that it would be something I would use and treasure for a long time. Last night when I was writing in it I opened up to the section on Loving Yourself that encouraged the reader to write a story or poem about self-acceptance, imagining that you are perfect, just the way you are. As soon as I started writing, all my thoughts poured out onto the paper. It was like I could no longer control what I was writing; the words just came out in the whole, naked truth. I ended up with this poem, and I thought that I should send it to you.

A Change

This morning when I woke up,
I sensed that something changed.
But it was nothing I could see,
Nothing was rearranged.
For some unexplainable reason,
When I looked into the mirror,
Even though the image was the same,
I could see myself a little clearer.
My hair was just as frizzy,
But it didn't matter, it's just hair.
And I still had curves in all the wrong places,
But for some reason I didn't care.
Then there were my braces.
They beautifully shone in the light.
And for once I liked my freckles,
Though I never imagined I might.
For once I felt just perfect,
Like I finally looked the part.
And I realized the change wasn't outside,
But, rather, in my heart.

Mary Davis

Today when I went to school, I seemed to have a whole new aura about myself, a self-confidence that I never knew was there before. I guess I finally realized that I don't have to be perfect for anybody else but me, and once I have that for myself, others will start to see me differently as well. I can already see that this journal is going to make a big impact on my life, and I just would like to thank you for that.

Sincerely,

Mary Davis

2

OVERCOMING OBSTACLES

People are like stained-glass windows.
They sparkle and shine when the sun is out,
but when the darkness sets in, their true beauty
is revealed only if there is a light from within.

Elisabeth Kübler-Ross

Never Count Me Out

I understand I am not perfect and life won't always wait for me. I say "life is what I make it!" I dream of tomorrow, not of yesterday. I try to be successful and bold and brave. I hope tomorrow creates a new foundation because I am young and making my own roads.

Deanna Seay

Dear Chicken Soup for the Teenage Soul,

I am writing to thank you for your books. They have given me the confidence to overcome any obstacle—and I have faced a lot of them. My mom tells me I am the kind of person who has always had plenty of challenges, and when I didn't encounter enough I could be counted on to create some of my own.

My first challenge was not self-chosen, however. I was born with my umbilical cord wrapped around my neck. I wasn't breathing. After the doctors were able to resuscitate me, they discovered that something else was wrong. My right leg was twice the size of my left one, with barely any muscle tissue. They assured my mother that it was not too serious and that it would eventually work itself out and grow to the size of a "normal" leg. Unfortunately, it never did.

When I was in sixth grade, my family moved to Washington State. Adjusting to the move was difficult enough, yet suddenly I was experiencing back pain that wouldn't go away. I saw a doctor who took X rays and noticed something very uncommon. My spinal cord had attached to a piece of tissue that was pulling my back out of alignment. It would require surgery.

The surgery was agonizing. It was a complicated procedure, and I went through a lot of pain. The doctors found nerve endings that were damaged, and for some reason I lost the ability to urinate and had to be hooked up to a catheter. It was one of the most unpleasant experiences I have ever faced and one I never could have gotten through without the support of my family. They were always by my side.

After the surgery, I had to slowly regain mobility in my legs. The nurses and my mom would help me to slowly walk the halls until I could walk further and further every day. I was determined to grow strong once again. Finally, they sent me home.

I was told that I was going to need help walking for a while, but I wasn't about to just accept that as the final word. The first morning I woke up in my own bed, I decided I wasn't going to need anybody's help. I wanted to go downstairs and say good morning to my mom—on my own. I swung my legs to the side of my bed, and I fell to the floor. I pulled myself up and walked to the stairs, holding onto the walls for support. When I reached the stairs I told myself there was no going back. I held onto the railing and slowly walked down the steps, one at a time. Finally, I reached the bottom. When my mom saw me, she was so shocked and so proud that she started crying. It was in that moment that I decided I would never let my physical challenges get in the way of my accomplishments.

Much to my parents' chagrin, as my physical therapy sessions were coming to a close my football career was just getting started. I had always wanted to play football, but when I found myself all padded up for my first practice I was terrified. I almost quit. I made it through practice that day, though, and when I got home my dad had me watch the movie Rudy with him. It is about a guy who beats all the odds against him to become a star football player at the University of Notre Dame. That movie changed my life.

I'm now sixteen and have been playing for our high school team, despite my physical challenges and my size. I am only 5'3" and 125 pounds, so I'm not much of an offensive threat. My coach lets me play in the games, though, and I've had so much fun with my teammates. My hard work and determination has earned me their respect, and they've even taken to calling me "Rudy." My goal is to attend Notre Dame and play on their football team. I hope they call me "Rudy."

Your books with stories of triumph and busting through barriers have reinforced my determination to get the most out of my life. Thank you for showing me that we all have within us the power to achieve beyond our wildest imaginations.

Sincerely,

Dan Mulhausen

Kind Words

That's when I learned the most important lesson I will probably learn in my life: One person can make a difference.

Laura Snell

Dear Ms. Kirberger,

It is very difficult for me to talk about this. I have never really shared my feelings about this with anyone, but I really feel I need to. Like any teenager my life revolved around my friends. I was busy going to parties, seeing movies, having sleepovers with my girlfriends and worrying about the pettiest things. I was a normal teen despite a rough beginning.

I was born with a number of heart complications. These complications required different operations throughout my life, especially within my first few years. My situation was life-threatening but, with the help of excellent medical care, I was able to survive. I have lived my whole life with this heart condition, so I'm comfortable with it. I'm not able to do everything my peers can, but I know my limits and live within them. My friends have always been aware of my medical history, and it has never come between our friendships. I have always lived a fairly normal life like everyone else my age . . . until recently.

Last year my mother noticed I was constantly tired and took me to the doctor as a precaution. My doctor noticed I had poor color. I had never taken the time to stop and notice these changes in myself. I was going to bed earlier and waking up tired. Blood tests showed I was low in iron, which seemed to be a reasonable explanation for my loss of energy and poor color.

As the weeks passed, I started experiencing cramps in my stomach. They progressively got worse and worse. I was reassured that iron, which I was now taking to bring up my red blood cell count, was hard on the stomach and it was a normal side effect. I continued the iron and dealt with the pains in my stomach. I returned to the doctor after a period of time, hoping to hear how the iron had improved my body. Instead of my hemoglobin rising, it had fallen for reasons unknown to all of us at the time. I was sent to different specialists around the city to help find answers for my situation. I received blood test after blood test.

The doctors still had no definite answers for me. Soon they were talking about a bone marrow test. I was scared and, for the first time in a long time, worried. In the past, I always knew I would get better, but now it was different. I wasn't sure I'd ever be better. It got to the point where I was walking around hunched over because of the horrible pain. I could not go out with my friends. I would get up in the morning and go lie down on the couch with a hot water bottle. That seemed to be how I spent my days.

My pains worsened. The school year was over, and I was looking forward to sleepover camp. I was so excited to be able to see all of my camp friends that I don't normally see during the year and have a change of environment. I was determined to leave home for camp despite my pains. However, my parents told me I would not be able to attend summer camp that year. I was extremely upset and I didn't want to hear of it, even though deep down I knew it was not possible for me to go in my condition. I remember saying to my mother the first night of the camp session, "If I were well, I'd be sleeping in a bunk bed tonight." She turned and said to me with tears in her eyes, "Kareny, I wish you were in a bunk bed tonight, too." I knew it hurt my parents to see me in pain and having to miss out on all the fun I should have been having that summer.

After more and more tests, seeing more doctors and being challenged by more pain, I was seen by a gastroenterologist at Sick Children's Hospital. I was finally given a diagnosis: Crohn's disease. It wasn't life-threatening like my heart, but it would affect my everyday quality of life. Believe it or not, the news came as a relief to my family and me. Sure, I was upset about what was happening to me. I had to make difficult changes in my life in order to get better, but at least now they knew what was wrong with me and I could follow the right path to feeling better again. I was given a steroid medication along with some antibiotics that were supposed to give me some quick relief. I went home from the hospital hoping and thinking I would be feeling better soon. Unfortunately, that wasn't the case. The medication wasn't helping, and I was having even more extreme pain. It got so bad that I was taken to the hospital by ambulance and admitted to the ward. I was taken off all food and given an IV. The IV failed to work. At this point,

I was really depressed. I felt awful. Nothing was working. I was so discouraged. I couldn't see myself ever getting better.

A tube-feeding treatment was now introduced. Of course, the idea of inserting a tube down my nose, into my throat and to my stomach was not ideal and was very hard for my family and me, but I tried it anyway. The treatment actually worked, and I eventually learned to insert the tube myself. I continued my nightly feedings through the tube for the next six months.

I wasn't having pains anymore, just the odd discomfort. I only did the tube feedings at night and overall I was so much better, but it was still difficult going back to school and seeing my friends. I had lost over twenty pounds. I still wasn't able to eat anything, and it was hard for me to concentrate.

I was doing better, but my medication gave me many side effects. My face retained water, which made me look extremely fat. I knew the kids at school noticed, but most were polite and didn't say anything. My friends were so supportive of me. I couldn't have asked for a better group of friends, but I could sense that things were uncomfortable for them. My face had become so fat that I didn't even recognize myself. I didn't want to go out with them because of this and many other reasons.

I started to eat a few solid foods again, but

seeing my friends binge on candy and french fries pushed me away from them. I had been through so much that summer. I felt twenty years older because of what I had struggled through. I had to be mature about things. My friends were worrying about movies, boys and themselves, much of what I worried about before I got sick. Now my whole life revolved around Crohn's disease, feeling good and keeping a positive mental attitude. I felt that I couldn't really relate to them anymore even though they had been so good to me. I was pushing myself away from them and as I pushed away, they thought I didn't want to be with them and they pushed away from me. I missed my friends and old life so much.

As the months passed, I lowered my medication and started to look like myself again. Things were getting better. I was feeling good and tried to make more of an effort to be a kid again and just hang out with my friends. I was starting to feel more in the loop of things, and one friend of mine contributed to that in the largest way. As we were walking out to recess one day, she turned to me and said, "You know what, Karen? After all that you have been through this year, I think it's so great that you can still laugh and joke with us." Just those few lines meant the world to me. That changed everything. For the first time I felt a friend understood how hard things had been for me and recognized how difficult it was for me to return to being a friend who could laugh and joke. I realized then that I didn't want to push away from my friends any longer. I wanted to be the person I used to be—the one who could kick back and have a good time.

Now, a year later, I'm feeling great and have returned to my normal self and my old life. I have triumphed over the barrier that held me back from being happy. A positive attitude, determination and a few special words from a special friend can really make a difference. This past year, I was lost and this friend helped to find me and return me to my life. I doubt she knew what an impact her words had on me, but I will never forget them. To that special friend of mine, I thank her and I love her.

Thank you for letting me share this with you, and hopefully other teens will be able to read this and know how important a few kind words can be.

Sincerely,
Karen

A Healed Heart

It's not about losing the memories, but gaining the strength to let go.

Jessica Leal

Dear Chicken Soup for the Teenage Soul,

I've always thought the name *Chicken Soup for the Soul* was cute and creative. However, I was unconvinced as to whether or not these books could really "heal" the soul. Don't get me wrong. I loved the stories in the *Chicken Soup* books, but I always just thought of them as light, heartwarming reading—until I broke up with my boyfriend of two years and discovered their true healing powers.

Brendan was my first serious boyfriend. I adored him. He didn't just have interests in life; he had passions. He loved to sing and play soccer. He was one of the funniest guys I had ever met. He had many friends and was very loyal to all of them. Most of all, he had goals for his life. I think these ambitions are what initially attracted me to him. He made me feel like I, too, could dream big.

When we first met in eighth grade, I hated his guts. He was annoying. All he ever talked about was this girl in our class, Tara, whom he had a crush on. He had followed her around for months trying to get a date until she finally agreed. He was ecstatic—and then she proceeded to publicly dump him two hours later. I felt sorry for him, and I let him talk to me throughout the whole ordeal. Over the next couple weeks we really got to know each other. And soon we were an item.

I smiled so much those first few months that I probably created wrinkles that will come back to haunt me when I'm fifty! I was in love. My friends told us all the time how cute we were together. I couldn't have agreed more. It wasn't always smooth sailing, but we always learned from our little quarrels and disagreements. The rough spots actually brought us closer together and made us grow. We were happy for two years.

A couple weeks before our two-year anniversary, Brendan started acting strange and distant toward me. I got a little worried, but I just figured we would get through it with a little effort, as always. A couple of days later I found out that I had mono. I was tired all the time and didn't feel like doing much of anything except sleeping. Talk about bad timing. Just when our relationship needed all the attention I could give it, all I could do was sleep. I missed four weeks of school and during that time Brendan and I grew farther and farther apart. I started hearing rumors about him and Tara from our mutual friends. Finally one night I called him to talk about our relationship. I told him I thought that it might be time to end things between us. He agreed. And we were no longer a couple. I cried and cried that night and spent at least four hours sobbing on the phone with my best friend, Lindsay. I couldn't believe it was over.

Over the next few weeks, I was really depressed. I couldn't get over him. I kept telling Lindsay how much I still liked him and how much I missed him. I must have driven her crazy, but she was so patient and kept giving me subtle advice and kind words. One day at school she handed me a bag and told me to open it when I got home. In the bag was her copy of *Chicken Soup for the Teenage Soul* flagged with personal notes from her on the stories she recommended. She also gave me a blank diary with this simple message written on the inside cover: "Who said being a teenager was easy?" Included in the package was also a heartfelt note that said she was there for me and that she wanted to help however she could. She told me that although I didn't believe it now, someday it wouldn't hurt me to think of him. Someday I wouldn't cry every time I looked at pictures of us. Someday I would remember our time together with a smile. Someday I would be over him.

Sure enough, as time wore on I slowly recovered. I let go of Brendan and learned to smile again. I later thanked Lindsay for all of her thoughtfulness and told her how much it had helped me. She said that someone had once helped her, too, and that I could repay her by helping someone else who needs it in the future. Since then I have been there for two of my closest friends through tough periods in their lives. A little *Chicken Soup,* some sticky notes and a few kind words from the heart can go a long way to make a friend feel better.

Thank you for creating the *Chicken Soup for the Teenage Soul* books. They are definitely the rattiest books on my shelf—well-read and well-borrowed— and have gone a long way to help heal the hearts of many.

Sincerely,
Jackie Johnstone

You'll Never Walk Again

Dear Teenage Chicken Soup,

My name is Nikie Walker. I am sixteen years old. I'm pretty much like any other sixteen-year-old. I was really involved with my high school, and very much liked by all of my peers. I was elected into many presidential clubs at my school. My mom was always saying that she never saw me. I was either running off to school, work, training or at practice. But, somehow I managed to keep my grades up and stay out of trouble.

On the morning of October 27, 1999, I was off to school early for a student council meeting. I had pulled out of the driveway and proceeded down the road. I was about eight hundred feet from my driveway when a dog ran out of the ditch beside me. My first reaction was that it was a child, so I tapped my brakes. (I was only going about twenty-five miles per hour.) My road happens to be very rough, and I was on loose gravel. Well, my car started to slide and face the other way. I hit a patch of pavement, which flipped my car two and a half times, landing on its roof. I had my seat belt on, but it broke during the first roll, and I suffered a broken back and a crushed spinal cord. I was paralyzed from the waist down.

At the hospital, I underwent a six-hour surgery. That night I was told that I would never walk again. I was devastated. I had always been so active, and now I was confined to a wheelchair.

While I was in the hospital, my grandma and my aunt bought me the first two volumes of *Chicken Soup for the Teenage Soul* and the *Journal*. I read them every night before I went to sleep. After reading all of the encouraging stories, I became determined to prove the doctors wrong. On December 13, I started therapy. I walked five steps that day! I improved as each day passed. Today, I am walking more than one hundred feet. The doctors are putting me in the medical books as a miracle. And I have these books to thank. Without an encouraging story every night of someone who was brave enough to fight against the odds, I probably would not be walking at all today. My next goal is to dance at my prom on May 13! I will reach that goal, thanks to you. I really appreciate your words of encouragement! They have made a big impact in my life.

Love always,
Nikie Walker

[*Editors' Note*: We received the following update from Nikie about her prom.]

Dear Chicken Soup for the Teenage Soul,

I am so happy to say that I made it to my junior prom and it was such a blast. My boyfriend, Adam, looked stunning in his little tuxedo. What started out as a frantic evening with all the pictures and making sure family and friends were able to see us, settled down once we were at the prom. The first song of the evening was "Wonderful Tonight," which was our prom's theme, but also happened to be Adam's and my song. He helped me out of my chair and we danced, standing up, for the whole song. It was magical! I tried to dance as much as I could standing up, but I would get tired so I danced the rest of the time sitting in my wheelchair. My friends would gather around me, joining hands with each other and dance with me in a giant circle. Adam did the sweetest thing and sat in one of the chairs from our table and danced with me so that we could be at the same level with each other. All of my friends, especially my boyfriend, really made my junior prom an unforgettable evening.

Thanks again,

Nikie

Winning Life's Battles

Dear Jack, Mark and Kimberly,

From reading the *Chicken Soup* books I have learned that we are all important and that we can *all* make a difference. You don't have to be a celebrity or superhero to have an impact on another person's life. I have been able to relate to so many of the stories in the *Teenage Soul* series and have learned a great deal about myself through reading them. I realized that I, too, have a story to tell, a story that might make another teen feel that much less alone.

The older I get, the more I realize how many people struggle with all types of problems in life. The media focuses on gangs, drugs or violence, but there is a different kind of struggle going on today—less talked about, but just as difficult for those involved. For myself and other disabled teenagers, we fight the battle to survive, the battle to be an individual in a society that can be less-than-accepting of "differences."

When I was five years old I was diagnosed with gastroenteritis and became a prisoner of the medical world, enduring restricted diets and intravenous treatments. I was too young to know the meaning of these words—but there was one issue I did understand and that was the pain of it all. Several years later, I was diagnosed with a debilitating orthopedic disorder that has left me confined to crutches for the past year.

My parents tried to give me the best life possible, but they could not cure the inquisitive stares of my peers. As I grew older, life became harder. I could not eat like everyone else, and I couldn't play with my peers. Teachers would complain because I was often out ill. People laughed at me. No one understood me. I tried to be strong, but I was usually left feeling like I was in my own little world, alone with no friends in sight.

In an effort to gain control of my body and my illness, I began to search for information about my condition. The Internet became my place of refuge, a place where I wasn't forced to show my face and be subjected to my daily dose of teasing. I found a group that accepted me, run by an Ohio teenager suffering from osteosarcoma. The group shared our triumphs and tribulations, and the chat room became our place to "get it all out." We shared stories of being blocked on the sidewalks by older students who called us names like "gimp" or "liar." The members of the group slowly grew stronger, and soon we were laughing about the same incidents that had once brought us to tears.

Most of the time, I have remained a fighter, but sometimes life gets me to the point where I can't take it anymore. I fight against being a statistic. According to the *Journal of the American Medical Association*, four thousand teenagers are diagnosed with depression every year as a result of their disabilities. I try hard not to become one of them.

With the help of groups such as the one I found on the Internet, disabled teenagers from around the world have been able to pull themselves above the daunting cries of ignorant peers. We are learning from each other that everyone deserves a chance to be known for what's on the inside and not only their physical appearance.

The hand that I have been dealt has made me stronger than my peers. I am a fighter. I am brave, mature and intelligent. I am a survivor. I am an advocate for children with disabilities. I am always pushing to make a difference.

I have finally realized that it is okay to be

different. It is okay to be an individual. Your books have taught me that I am important and I, too, have a story to tell. I am a fighter and a survivor. I am me.

Sincerely,

Rachel A. Morgan

[*Editors' Note:* Rachel shared with us an Internet resource she recommends for disability awareness: *Band-Aides and Blackboards*—a Web site dedicated to growing up with medical problems. *http://funrsc. fairfield.edu/~jfleitas/contents.html*]

Books that Rachel recommends include:

1. Bethy and the Mouse: A Father Remembers His Children with Disabilities. *Donald C. Bakely, Brookline Books, Inc., April 1997.*
2. Dancing in the Rain: Stories of Exceptional Progress by Parents of Children with Special Needs. *Annabel Stehli, Georgiana Organization, Inc., November 1995.*
3. Anna: A Daughter's Life. *William Loizeaux, Arcade Publishing, Inc., February 1993.*
4. Until Angels Close My Eyes. *Lurlene McDaniel, Bantam Doubleday Dell Books, June 1998.*

Yes I Can

Dear Chicken Soup for the Teenage Soul,

I am writing to tell you how much I have enjoyed your books. The stories of courage have really touched and moved me. They made me realize that I, too, have an important story to tell and one that might inspire teens to try harder and to be grateful for what they have. I hope my story can help another teen through these trying years. Through my writing I feel I have been able to help *myself* discover who I really am and who I aspire to be.

Sincerely,
Kerri Meulemans

Oh, Yes I Can

Name-brand clothing, fitting in, living up to the stereotype of who everyone else thinks you are— these are the things that concern the typical teen- ager. The strand of commonality that binds all teenagers together is the longing to meet the expecta- tions of their peers and gain the precious prize of acceptance.

Throughout my teenage years I made a point to strive for this so-called acceptance, and to fulfill my desperate desire to belong. But I had an extra obstacle to over- come; I was different.

At birth I was diagnosed with a cranio-facial dis- order called Treachers Collins Syndrome. The syn- drome is characterized by faulty, undeveloped bone structure in the facial region, and hearing impairment. The syndrome is very rare, and researchers have yet to find a cure. The expectations for my successful future were minimal, my potential diminished. I was another statistic without a cure, another nameless subject of research.

But my parents were not about statistical data. They made sure I received all the best care and attention, both medically and emotionally. I became the youngest patient my doctor ever fitted for a hearing aid. After I came to understand that the hearing aid was not a pacifier, I was on the road to progress. I had the best speech specialists who worked with me in my early years, thus not only helping me to keep up with peers but eventually to surpass them intellectually. Throughout grade school, I was an A student, defying those who said I wasn't capable to be in the same classroom as the other students. I ignored the skeptics and not only excelled academically, but found it in myself to join extracurricular activities and meet those standards, as well.

In high school, I enrolled in advanced placement courses and made the honor roll. I played tennis and was even creative editor for our school newspaper in an attempt to establish groundwork for my future career as a journalist.

I am now embarking on my senior year of high school. I will not only graduate, but will graduate early because of my fierce determination in defying the system.

Maybe I didn't always fit the typical teenage mold; maybe I wasn't who everyone else thought I should be. But I know more about myself and who I am at seventeen than most people will discover about themselves in their entire lifetime. After approximately twenty reconstructive surgeries, and more yet to come, I have realized I need to live for who I want to be, not who society thinks I should be. Had I given in to the pressures, I wouldn't be where I am today.

I had people who believed in me, so I believed in myself. These people, my parents, shone the light at the end of the tunnel for me. I now have the confidence to leap over obstacles without fear of those who underestimate me. I can be whoever and whatever I desire to be. So what if I started out different. So what if I'm hearing impaired. I could still be the next Miss America.

Kerri Meulemans

Getting the Most Out of Life

I have gone through many difficult experiences in my life, barely squeezing around the obstacles in my way. But with those challenges came a great deal of learning. If I had to go back and do it all over again, I would not change a single thing. What I have come to learn is too valuable.

Marissa Angel

Dear Authors of
Chicken Soup for the Teenage Soul,

I love your books! They are so wonderful! When I started the first *Teenage Soul*, I was going through a really hard, depressing time, and suicide had popped into my head more than once. I read the stories about teenagers who had committed suicide, or attempted suicide, and they really made me think. I realized how incredibly stupid it would be for me to end my life for my own selfish reasons, just so I didn't have to face my problems and reality. I would have hurt so many people who love me. I thank you from the bottom of my heart for making me wake up and face my reality.

I'm fifteen years old, and I have cystic fibrosis. It's not contagious—I was born with it. This disease affects the lungs, the respiratory system and the digestive tract. I have been in the hospital several times, and it can be a lonely feeling. A part of me has felt alone all my life because of this disease. Sometimes my friends say, "Oh, I understand," but they don't really. No matter how hard they try, or how hard they want to, they can't understand what it's like to live with a life-threatening disease. I'm lucky, though: On the outside you can't tell anything is wrong with me. Some people with this disease aren't as lucky because they can look anorexic. Some die young, in their twenties. I am a very healthy cystic fibrosis kid. Sometimes I even forget I have it, but other times I can't help but be reminded.

During one of my first stays in the hospital, I made friends with a girl my age who had cancer. I remember her shiny bald white head in contrast to her bright blue hospital gown. We played together all the time, racing down the hospital corridors on our IV poles, kinda like scooters. The nurses would just laugh and let us have fun. I can't remember exactly why, but she went away and we didn't see each other anymore.

Later, I was moved to a different room. I shared it with another CF girl, Kate, who was sicker than I was. Even though I was in the hospital, the time we spent together was one of the best times of my life. It was cool just to have someone like me with the same illness. We would take our medicine together and have therapy together. She taught me how to blow smoke rings out of my nebulizer. We spent an endless amount of hours just talking and hanging out with one another. Our friendship was special. My health eventually improved, and I was able to go home. Kate was not so fortunate. She had to remain in the hospital. I lost contact with her after I left the hospital. The following summer I found out she had died. I was so sad not knowing how she died—or if she died alone. The whole time I was in the hospital I never really saw anyone come visit her, maybe a telephone call once in a while but that was it. She was only fourteen when she died. When I think about it sometimes it scares me to know that she died at fourteen and I am now fifteen. I get this lonely feeling that sometimes smothers me. None of my friends have to think about or wonder if they will live to see their sixteenth birthday. I do, almost every day. I think about Kate and the fact that she will never get to drive or freak out over SATs. She will never marry or have kids. I live in two worlds—one of which is very lonely and scary. But no matter how lonely or scary it may seem, I will survive. I've promised myself many times that I will live to see another day.

Today I enjoy playing soccer for my high school team. I long jump and throw the javelin. I act, sing and dance. I love to read and write, and I live my life to the fullest. From reading your books, I have learned that it's possible to do anything you want to, and that everyone is made of "Tough Stuff."

Sincerely,

Emily R. Monfort

Regaining My Pride

Dear Chicken Soup for the Teenage Soul,

About a year ago, I bought *Chicken Soup for the Teenage Soul* and the *Journal*. I felt a little weird buying the books because, first of all, I'm not much into self-help books. And second of all, I'm not a teenager anymore—I'm twenty-one years old. But I realized that these books aren't really about self-help; rather, they're "self-inspiring."

When I bought the journal I filled it out completely. In many ways, it has helped me to get over and put to rest a lot of things that were upsetting me about my life. I was finally able to move on from situations I'd been stewing over for years. One situation in particular has plagued me, but by writing about it in the journal I realize

I am a better person for having gone through it. That was a big step for me.

I started twelfth grade in the fall of 1995. It was supposed to be the best year of my life. I was finally going to graduate from high school. Over the next twelve months I was going to be taking steps toward my future. I applied for college and a ton of scholarships.

Unfortunately, I was struggling terribly in my history class. I ended up dropping it with only two weeks to go in the semester. My guidance counselor assured me that everything would be fine, as long as I passed all my other finals. I was so happy that day. I felt like I could conquer anything.

Finally graduation day came and the principal spoke those cherished words: "We now present to you the graduating class of nineteen hundred ninety-six." When I heard those words I knew I was really doing it; I was heading to college. Or at least I thought I was—until I received my transcripts in the mail.

I opened the envelope that would confirm that I had officially graduated from high school, and my knees buckled. I could not find my voice. I had missed graduating by one credit, my history credit. I had trusted my guidance counselor. I was devastated.

I spent the next month losing my dreams and

losing myself. The walls around me started caving in, and I constantly wondered when they would stand up again. I was terrified of having to go back to high school, having to face everyone who would know that I was a failure. I was not prepared to move backwards. I had waited for so long for a new beginning, a new way of life. I hated the thought of being left behind while everyone else got to go out and discover new worlds in college. I was miserable.

But I started high school again in the fall and things actually started looking up. I finished in November. It was a shock to be back in school, but suddenly my life seemed to make a 180-degree turn. I made some new friends who have turned out to be lasting and unforgettable. They took me in and made me feel at home, and that gave me the strength to move on. I rediscovered my identity and came to the realization that I was going to be all right; I was really going to make it. The feeling of loss finally subsided.

I finally took that big step and went to college in the fall of 1997—a year after the rest of my class. College has been everything I dreamed of and hoped for. I am proud of the person I am today, and I am that person because I swallowed my pride and went back to high school.

Thank you for your books—and for helping me

to discover that the obstacles I've faced in my life have also been my most profound learning opportunities.

Sincerely, a devoted fan,

Crystal McHargue

The Shadow

Dear Teenage Chicken Soup,

I am a nineteen-year-old student from Canada. I battled with anorexia nervosa for nearly seven years and I can now say I am well on my way to recovery. During my slow recovery period, I was able to express my feelings and emotions through writing. Your books have helped me through this process. I have enclosed a poem that really sums up what I was feeling. The title is "Shadowland" and it is the word I coined to describe my life as a student and athlete with anorexia nervosa.

Anorexia is an illness that I have struggled with for many years, one that has jeopardized my life and has even placed me in the hospital. You see, I believe that, in essence, developing an eating disorder is akin to becoming a shadow of one's former self. My experience with anorexia has been a transformation into a silent, thin, gray and flattened body that I call my shadow. In the worst of times, I have felt haunted by this figure lurking behind me, one that, despite my best efforts, I have been unable to free myself from. For years, I have struggled to achieve my many ambitious academic and athletic goals, feeling as though I carry the weight of the world on my shoulders. Anorexia, for me, has been like a journey through a world of shadowy gray.

I have no doubt that many of you are wondering what could possibly drive young and enthusiastic individuals who once belonged to the "real world" down such a dangerous path of self-destruction. I am aware that many images portrayed in the media are the driving force behind a North American dieting industry based on cruel, contradictory and unrealistic ideals. I do not, however, hold them completely responsible for the increasing number of young people who suffer from severe eating disorders today. I believe that the cause of these debilitating illnesses is one that is much deeper than the desire to resemble the models in leading fashion magazines. Contrary to popular belief, people with anorexia are not always vain, frivolous and attention-seeking individuals who feel that their lives would be enhanced if they lost a few pounds.

Rather, the skeletal and "shadowlike" physical appearances of people suffering from anorexia are silent manifestations of the difficulty they experience in coping with a wide array of daily pressures. These are stresses that other people may not display the same degree of sensitivity towards, or if they do, handle them in different ways. In my opinion, anorexia is a way of not feeling, of starving until the dull numbness of the "Shadowland" sets in. In this state, victims of anorexia are too starved to feel the frightening consequences of having to deal with issues like relationships, family life, change and responsibility.

Enclosed is a poem I wrote. I hope you will publish it, as it is my deepest desire to know that my words can help others the way your books have helped me.

Yours truly,

F.J.M.

The Shadowland

She is wire
Easily bent and twisted
And molded and shaped by uncaring hands
She's a coat hanger under the clothes

She's a bird in a gilded cage
Her screams only faintly heard
Unable to fly with one broken wing
She patiently waits for a key

And with eyes like a dried-up wellspring
She is blinded by unshed tears
Too terrified to let even one fall
Lest others should sense imperfection

Her most recent purchase was at the "Gap Kids"
Although she is sixteen years old
Waif-like and innocent, shrunken breasts, hips and thighs
She patiently waits for a key

Undeserving of life's simple pleasures
Seized by terror when she opens her mouth
Jaws bound and clenched, hammered with fear
She recently forgot how to chew

Intent to secure her shrunken self
She learned how to lie in a day
With a cross of her fingers behind her back
She falsely proclaims that she ate

And isn't it strange to talk to
An anatomical representation of skull?
Transparent skin that barely contains
Her delicate package of bones

And only when voices that care sound louder
Than the person who lives in the mirror
Will this hollow-eyed former shadow of self
Summon the courage to grow

The puzzling paradox of the hunger disease
Scales that taunt and reflections that scream
A magical number determines the worth
Of this slave to the gods of perfection.

F.J.M.

Discovering Me

Dear Chicken Soup for the Teenage Soul,

I'm probably not the first person to write you guys a letter like this, but after reading *Chicken Soup for the Teenage Soul* something inside of me wanted to share a little part of my life with you.

For most people, life has its ups and downs, but dealing with the down times can be especially brutal. I was having one of those down times just after entering my first year of high school. Going in I was filled with great anticipation that the next four years of my life would be golden ones. I don't know, maybe it was from watching too many episodes of *Saved by the Bell,* but I thought I was totally prepared by having "grown and matured" in junior high. In my mind, I thought I already had most of the answers to life, but once I settled into my new environment I was faced with a rude awakening. My peers, whom I fully expected to embrace me, distanced themselves from me instead. It didn't seem to matter that I was friends with some of these people before high school began. I realized we were all making a big transition, but I never thought this would happen. I was crushed and confused. I felt miserable and alone. I put up a front for my peers, teachers and parents, not wanting how I was really feeling to be seen, especially since I was surrounded by others who thought that depression that lasted more than two hours was weird.

This is not to say that I was always unhappy. There were definitely times of happiness, insight and hope, but more times than not I wanted to crawl into a hole and hide. I had been used to having the best grades, the best friends and being recognized for my talents in almost anything I did. But now I felt uncared for and invisible, like I didn't even exist. It brought on feelings of insecurity, and I became paranoid that everyone was talking about me behind my back.

Slowly I began to realize that it isn't what life brings to you, it is what you bring to your own life. That painful lesson took me a while to learn. I would look with envy at other people's lives. It seemed they were filled with laughter, close friends and popularity. I would ask myself with bewilderment, *Why can't that be my life?*

Eventually I was able to regain my composure. I started my sophomore year with a clean slate. I felt much more comfortable with myself and didn't care so much about what others thought of me. I stopped wishing for lifestyles that weren't mine and started being grateful for what I did have. I made new friends who were new to my school that year. I began to see how many of the girls I had once envied were always talking behind each other's backs, and I realized that nothing is ever as perfect as it seems. I began doing things I loved, such as taking dance classes and acting in school plays. The more I did, the better I felt about myself and the closer I got with my friends. When I came across the quote, "God grant me the serenity to accept the things I cannot change, the courage to change the things I can, and the wisdom to know the difference," it summed up a lot of what I was searching for.

One day I picked up a copy of *Chicken Soup for the Teenage Soul* that was lying on my friend's dresser and began to read it. The stories were so inspiring that I borrowed it and spent the next week reading the rest before I bought a copy of my own. The wonderfully uplifting stories and poems made me feel so much less alone in the world and in my experiences. They taught me that there was so much more I could do to become a better person. They reminded me how far a simple act of kindness can go, and not to compare myself with others, but to compare myself to me. *Chicken Soup* taught me that no matter how far you think you've come, there's always a next step. There's always more kindhearted people to meet and new experiences that lie ahead, and all we have to do is look for them. Thanks so much for caring!

Yours truly,

Lauren Mark

Not Alone

Dear Chicken Soup,

I'm entering my senior year in high school. I'm approaching college and getting ready to leave behind many rough memories of my high school days.

My struggles started in seventh grade when I began passing out. I had various tests done to see why. I was told I had low blood pressure, which causes a rapid heartbeat. I tested many medications and finally found one that helped. My average blood pressure was about 80/60 on a good day. To this day, I continue to battle this problem.

Then, two years ago, I was diagnosed with fibromyalgia, a muscle disease that is not really helped by medication. It's like having a pulled muscle and when your muscles flare up, it can last as long as three months. There are eighteen points in the body where it can occur. I have it in twelve of the eighteen points. I was bedridden for a month two years ago. Cold weather, rain, or physical or emotional stress can trigger the flare-ups.

It's hard enough to be a healthy teenager and go through the typical changes with friends, family, relationships, school, etc. Add to that missing two to three months of school a year, and it can make things very difficult. The hardest part was, on the outside I looked normal like everyone else; however, on the inside I was in horrible pain. Some teachers have passed judgment on me thinking that since my physical appearance is fine I must be okay. One teacher even told my class when I was absent one day that I was faking my heart problem. Those judgments hurt me more than anyone will ever know. I felt like I was always having to prove myself to everyone. I have lost friends, but I have also realized who my true friends really are.

I battled with depression as well, because I felt like an outsider, a freak, isolated from the rest of the world. I longed to be normal and healthy. I even developed an eating disorder. In the beginning, I had lost a lot of weight because of my heart condition. I went from a size eleven to a size six in one year. For the first time, I felt like I was attractive because I was skinny. I was receiving more attention than ever. I felt like people liked me more because I was skinny and that mindset was a large part of my eating problem. I would still feel depressed, though, because of all that was going on in my life, and I would eat a lot hoping the stress would go away. But then I would throw up the food so I would still look good. Eventually I overcame both these problems with the help of family, friends and a wonderful job.

My mother, who is an amazing woman, stuck by me and encouraged me in all my times of need. She has truly inspired me. She took the time to try and understand all that I was feeling and was there for me when I felt like I had no one. Having her believe in me helped me to believe in myself. She helped me get a job at the retirement home where she worked. I had grown up around this place but working there changed my life. To help these elderly people and see the sparkle of appreciation they got in their eyes was wonderful and motivating. I found a purpose knowing I had something to give to these people. I gained a confidence that was disassociated from my looks. I was loved by them unconditionally. This gave me the strength to overcome my depression and my eating disorder. This also helped open my eyes and see that my real friends didn't care if I was skinny or not; they loved me for who I was on the inside.

Life can be so overwhelming, but I feel much stronger now having overcome these obstacles. I have had plenty of time to dig deep into myself to find the person I am. I have been able to figure out what I value in my life—that I don't need to prove myself if someone doesn't understand me. A goal in my life is to help other young people find positives in their lives even when faced with certain obstacles.

Your books have helped me to realize that I'm not alone in my struggles; that there are other people out there going through similar adversities. So many teenagers have found the strength they need in the stories in these books. I am hoping my story might do the same—that would make me feel good.

Sincerely,

Andrea Blake

Lucky After All

Dear Chicken Soup for the Teenage Soul,

I have been reading your books for a couple of years and have found great comfort in the stories of people overcoming adversity. Your books always put me in a good mood. They give me a bit of perspective on my own problems and the energy to live a "normal" teenage life. Over the last thirteen years, I have grown to accept myself for who I am. I am at the stage where I am comfortable with myself, but it was only two years ago when I was extremely concerned about my appearance.

At the young age of four, I was introduced to hearing aids. With nerve damage to my eardrums, my hearing was cut by 30 percent. During my early childhood, my parents noticed that I never played with my sister or brother and I never watched TV with them. They never really thought about it until one particular afternoon. I was about two years old, and our whole family was outside. I ran out onto the street and into oncoming traffic. My grandpa was calling to me, but I wasn't listening to him and I almost got hit by a car. That made my parents think. They insisted our doctor perform test after test until they determined that I was deaf.

The damage is the same in both ears, so my mom believes I was born with it. My dad, however, chooses to voice a different opinion. He thinks my nerves were damaged during my delivery, with the doctor's forceps. Either way, the damage is called sensorineural hearing loss, in which a deterioration of the inner ear is present. It will never get better, but it will never get worse either. I was searching on the Internet a year ago when I found out that this type of misfortune is irreversible. I cried quite a bit at first because a part of me always dreamed about the day when I could have an operation that would make me "normal." But in a way I expected it. I was sure that my audiologist would have mentioned the option had there been one.

Finding out my condition has no cure isn't the worst thing I have been through, however. Throughout my childhood, many kids have teased me. The worst memory I have is when I was in seventh grade, and a few boys were very loudly imitating the quiet "beep, beep" noise that my hearing aids make. I still remember calling my mom crying and begging her to come take me home.

That may have been a few years ago, but even today many people are still openly curious about "those strange things in your ears." A lot of people don't seem to understand that hearing loss is a physical health problem, not a mental health problem. I try very hard to make eye contact with anyone I am talking to, but their eyes always seem to wander off to one of my ears. This makes me feel very self-conscious so I will try to distract the person by turning my head, scratching my ear or shaking my hair over my ears so they have to look at me. Now I have started being more comfortable with exposing my ears out in the open. Last year I hardly ever wore my hair back in a ponytail because I thought people were looking. These days I'll still do the odd ear-scratch or head-turn to get people out of their daze, but not nearly as often.

Obviously there are many disadvantages to hearing aids. I can't swim or sleep with them. It is also extremely hard to hear in public gatherings and the classroom with all the background voices. Even with a group of friends, I find it difficult to follow the conversation at times. I often have to ask people to repeat what they say. But there is one huge advantage that I think I take for granted sometimes: being lucky enough to wear my hearing aids so that I can hear. I hate wearing the aids, but knowing that I am able to, and that my hearing is not going to get any worse makes me so happy. Another advantage that not too many people know about is being able to shut my aids off whenever I want. If I'm trying to concentrate on counting or reading, one quick, swift move and no one knows. My own personal silence. That's always fun.

Sure, I would like to be able to wear a hearing aid that is a little less noticeable than the one I wear today, but the most important thing is being able to hear as well as I can.

All my life my one wish was to just be a "normal" teenage girl. But since I have entered high school, that wish has changed. I have been getting good grades since I was in preschool. I have a great family, great friends and a boyfriend who is more than comfortable with my hearing aids. I play hockey and rugby, and I am able to work at my family's business. When you put it all together, I would have to say that I am pretty normal, after all.

Sincerely,

Tara Sangster

Inspired by Tragedy

Dear Chicken Soup for the Teenage Soul,

I am currently a senior in high school in Indonesia. As you may already know, the current situation in Jakarta, Indonesia, is not at its best. The government is struggling to develop a system of democracy that will serve the citizens of Indonesia and the country as a whole to the best of its ability. Economically, Indonesia is in terrible strife. Striving to change the once-corrupt government, the students (the future of Indonesia) fight for freedom of speech, human rights and equality. Last year our school was forced to end early because of the civil unrest in Jakarta. Students from our school were advised by their embassies to evacuate the country immediately. During this time, tensions were high and Indonesian students and citizens felt they had no control in this situation. In anger, they burned and looted many shops, department stores and buildings. Desperately trying to convey that the situation was under control, the Indonesian military was sent to ruthlessly kill and brutally batter many innocent civilians. We have experienced a tragic and horrific event that will no doubt go down in history.

Through this experience, I have felt inspired to write many poems that in some way connect to the situation in Indonesia. I want to share these poems with the world because I feel that the rest of the world deserves to know about what we, the entire population of Indonesia, have felt for so long. I do not claim to know what other people feel or the way that the situation has affected them. But I do know that many people have suffered and shed many tears over lost loved ones, and the hardships of striving to support a family on minimum wage and the traumas of living in a country that is trying to recover from a devastating experience. Below is a poem that I feel really describes the current situation in Jakarta. I would be so grateful to hear from you.

Sincerely,
Melanie Campbell

The Solid Sun Shines On

Pollution engulfs the once germ-free air
taking command.
Factories multiply without stop.
In the obscurity of night
lurks unsoundness of mind,
causing mishap and corruption.
Innocence is lost,
too fast to understand.
Poverty captures millions,
unwilling to let go.
Death's icy grasp
uncommunicative, uncontrollable,
knocks forcefully
at the door.
Yet children still dance
amongst purple poppy fields,
chase butterflies till dawn,
their laughter, never ceasing,
like silver bells ringing,
resounds throughout town.
Rain still falls,
clear droplets from the sky,
washing away the filth

so we may begin again.
Amidst all the wretched weeds,
there springs a flowering seed
of hope.

After the darkness of the night,
the solid sun shines on.

Melanie Campbell

3

THANK YOU!

To speak gratitude is courteous and pleasant,
to enact gratitude is generous and noble, but to
live gratitude is to touch Heaven.

Johannes A. Gaertner

Chicken Soup? How Lame!

Dear Chicken Soup,

The past few months have seemed to be the hardest time in my life! Just turning eighteen a month ago, my life has been filled with more changes and tough decisions than I thought existed.

A few days before my birthday, I was left with what seemed to be the biggest disappointment of my life. Only three people, besides me, knew of the situation—one being my little brother's girlfriend, who, by the way, is also one of my very best friends.

On my birthday, she handed me a slightly heavy gift bag, and said, "I was going to get you something else, but I think you need this more." Thinking it was the *Shakespeare's Romeo and Juliet* video with Leonardo DiCaprio that she knew I wanted so badly, I dug into the bag with eager anticipation. As I pulled it out, I slowly realized . . . *It's a book.* I thought to myself, "She knows how I hate to read." I never read anything unless it's absolutely necessary—schoolwork, letters, *Seventeen* and *YM* magazines (which are very necessary), or the instructions to an occasional box of hair dye (trust me, those are absolutely necessary!).

I smiled and said, "Thank you!" I think she sensed my attitude, because she quickly commented, "I know, you're thinking, *a book?* But my aunt bought me this book for Christmas and, trust me, you'll love it. Especially right now. I know it'll help you; that's why I bought you one."

Well, a few days went by, and I hadn't picked up the book. To tell you the truth, looking at that big, thick book kind of scared me. "It's going to take me forever to read that! *Chicken Soup?* How lame! I know, I can use it at night for my insomnia. I'm sure it'll put me to sleep!"

So, one night, I started reading it. Big mistake! After reading the very first story, "Losing the 'Us',"* I couldn't put it down! "How ironic! This girl went through exactly what I did. No way!" So I kept reading. "I can't believe other people have gone through what I have, and feel like I do!"

---

*"Losing the 'Us'," by Lia Gay, Chicken Soup for the Teenage Soul, pp. 3–5.

My life was still in the middle of the story, but with this book, I got to read the ending of many stories like my own. I told myself, "Even though it seems like I'm going through the worst right now, it will pass, and things will turn out better than I could have imagined. I'll be a better person for going through these trials."

Honestly, this book has truly changed my outlook on life completely. I no longer look at problems like, "Oh no! My life is absolutely falling apart!" I see a trial now and think, "I know this won't last forever. The question is, what can I learn from this to become a better person?"

From beginning to end, every story in this book is so touching! You can ask all my friends. I am one of the most unemotional people you could ever meet, but I have even cried at times.

Now, I recommend to all my friends that they *get this book!* It is an absolute must-have for every teenager!

Thank you, *Chicken Soup*, for making this book. It has a permanent place beside my bed on my end table. Thank you most of all, Kella, for giving me this priceless gift! It is the best birthday present I have ever received!

Love,
Cassandra Brady

Respecting Others

Dear Jack, Mark and Kim,

I am such a huge admirer of your books. They have literally changed my way of thinking and how I act. I never used to really think twice about making rude comments to people in my school who I thought were weird. I want to share how a story in your book changed the way I treat people.

When it comes to the social structure, my school, like most typical high schools, has all kinds of different groups of friends. My group of friends is a tight group, and we consider each other best friends. Unfortunately, someone always seems to get left out of a group and in our group that was Jessica. For some cruel reason we liked to make fun of her. We thought it was actually pretty hilarious. We constantly made jokes about the way she dressed and how her hair always looked like it was never clean. It wasn't that she didn't wash it, but there never seemed to be any life to it, like it was straw. We just couldn't figure it out. We would make up poems and silly little songs about her hair. We knew we were being immature, but it was a way to get a cheap laugh here and there, not really realizing what it could be doing to her inside.

One day, my English teacher read us a story from *Chicken Soup for the Soul* titled, "A Simple Gesture."* It was about a boy named Mark who was on his way home from school with all his books and everything else he had stored in his locker. He had fallen and a fellow classmate named Bill helped him up. Mark was going home to commit suicide because he was having a difficult time in school and in life in general. But because of Bill's kindness towards Mark, he decided not to hurt himself, realizing what other good things he might miss later on down the road. When she finished reading the story, I immediately thought about Jessica and what we were doing to her and how horrible she must feel when we make fun of her. It made me wonder if all the jokes we told about her caused her to think about suicide.

My next class with Jessica was in ten minutes and she sat in front of me. This was where we usually

---

"A Simple Gesture," by John W. Schlatter, Chicken Soup for the Soul, pp. 34–35.

made fun of her hair, but this time I didn't nor did I ever again. Instead, I wrote her a letter apologizing for the way I had treated her. I told her I couldn't apologize for the rest of the girls, and that maybe they just didn't realize yet what they were doing to her and the pain they were probably causing her. This letter was the most sincere apology I had ever given to anyone in my life. When I handed it to her she wanted to throw it away, but I stopped her and begged her to read it. She said, "Why, so I can just read all the insults that you wrote to me? I don't feel like putting up with this anymore." So I took the letter from her hands and started reading it out loud to her in front of the entire class. My friends gave me the strangest looks, but I didn't care at that point. I wanted them and the rest of the students to hear what I had written. When I came to the end of the letter I said, "I'm so sorry for what I've done to you. I hope that somehow you can find it in your heart to forgive me." She ran up to me with tears in her eyes and hugged me. I cried with her. I could see my friends whispering to each other, but it didn't matter.

I had gained a new friend that afternoon. I will always be forever grateful to my English teacher for reading us that story and to you for publishing such amazing stories. You have helped open my eyes and to realize that everyone deserves to be treated with respect, no matter what. Keep up the great work you guys are doing.

Sincerely,
Jennifer Lirette

A Plea for All of Us

Dear Kimberly,

My parents have been foster parents for over ten years, but for about the past five years we've taken in mostly teenagers. Many are pregnant teens or unwed moms. It hasn't always been easy, but it's always been worth it, and I've learned a lot about people over the last several years. One of the things that has benefited me the most is learning to see where people are coming from. It's much easier to love someone, and much harder to get hurt, if you can understand the reasons that people act the way they do—whether it's fear, pain, or just plain not knowing any better. I wrote this poem from the perspective of my foster sisters, but I believe that, to some degree, all of us can relate. Very few people show all of their true selves, and everyone is crying out for someone to care enough to see past the outer shell to what's really there behind it. This is a plea to all of us from everyone around us who is hurting. Thanks, Kimberly.

Sincerely,
Rachel N. Bentley

Stone by Stone

I have a wall you cannot see
Because it's deep inside of me.
It blocks my heart on every side
And helps emotions there to hide.
You can't reach in,
I can't reach out.
You wonder what it's all about.

The wall I built that you can't see
Results from insecurity.
Each time my tender heart was hurt
The scars within grew worse and worse.
So stone by stone
I built a wall
That's now so thick it will not fall.

Please understand that it's not you,
Continue trying to break through.
I want so much to show myself,
And love from you will really help.
So bit by bit
Chip at my wall,
Till stone by stone it starts to fall.

I know the process will be slow,
It's never easy to let go
Of hurts and failures long ingrained
Upon one's heart from years of pain.
I'm so afraid
To let you in.
I know I might get hurt again.

I try so hard to break the wall,
But seem to get nowhere at all.
For stone upon each stone I've stacked,
And left between them not a crack.
The only way
To make it fall
Are imperfections in the wall.

I did the best I could to build
A perfect wall, but there are still

A few small flaws, which are the key
To breaking through the wall, to me.
Please use each flaw
To cause a crack,
To knock a stone off of the stack.

For just as stone by stone was laid
With every hurt, with every pain;
So stone by stone the wall will break,
As love replaces every ache.
Please be the one
Who cares enough
To find the flaws, no matter what.

Rachel N. Bentley

Defining Courage

Dear Chicken Soup,

I work with emotionally and behaviorally disturbed teenage girls in a residential treatment center. The center has both editions of *Chicken Soup for the Teenage Soul*. I find them very useful when I am working with these girls. Sometimes a lesson has more impact if it is coming from a story about someone else. I have worked in this field for over three years now and have always admired the girls with whom I work. I often question who is learning more—the girls from myself or myself from the girls. They are survivors in the truest sense of the word. They come from homes and communities where they have been abused physically, sexually and verbally. They have repeatedly experienced that trusting others has had horrible outcomes, yet they try and try again to trust someone in the hopes of finding that person who will unconditionally accept them and believe in them. (And what a gift to have one of them trust you.)

They come into treatment and bare their souls to people they do not know that well. They learn that they are good, talented, brave and worthwhile people. They learn that trust is very special and not easily acquired. They learn that they are not to blame and they let go of the past. They begin to take responsibility for themselves and for their actions. Not only do they survive, but they seem to thrive in the face of adversity.

In this day and age, we always hear about the problems with kids today. It enrages me to hear this because I know otherwise. It is exactly that attitude that defeats "those kids" and holds them down. I am tired of hearing about today's youth in a negative way. The girls I work with fight a tremendous battle that most people will never know. They define courage and perseverance. I wish the rest of the world could understand how brave, resilient and amazing these young women are.

I am writing to you in dedication to these women and the many people who play a role in their survival. You have helped inspire them to tell their stories of triumph and to express themselves through their incredible poetry. They have melted my heart, made me cry and put a huge smile on my face, all at once. I would love to put you in touch with these amazing women so you can share their incredible beauty.

Sincerely,
Meridith A. Spencer

P.S. I have worked in two different locations of the agency I work for. When I left my last dormitory the girls made me my own *Chicken Soup* book, *Chicken Soup for the Tubman Soul* (I worked in the Tubman Dorm), filled with stories, poems and quotes from my time at the program. I treasure this gift as it truly came from their souls, and I proudly display it in my bedroom.

Coming Together

Dear Chicken Soup for the Teenage Soul,

My name is Jen, and I am nineteen years old. In September 1999 I left Sheffield, England, to live and volunteer at a place called Corrymeela in Northern Ireland. I am here for a year. The Corrymeela Community is a diverse community of people of all Christian traditions who are individually and collectively committed to the healing of social, religious and political divisions in Northern Ireland and throughout the world. I am joined by eleven other volunteers: six from Ireland and five from other parts of the world such as Sweden, America and Germany. Together with the permanent staff, they have become my work mates, support structure, friends and family, and the people I have grown to love. I live in a house on-site with the other volunteers. When I first set out for this adventure back in September, the idea of living with eleven complete strangers was a pretty strange thing to comprehend. Now that I have been living, eating, working and socializing with this group for close to a year, I can't imagine our paths not having crossed.

The groups I work with at Corrymeela consist of all different people who come by the hundreds every year to stay at the center. We see all types come through our doors: school groups, single parents, youth groups, families, churches, ex-prisoners, recovering alcoholics, you name it. Most of the people we work with come from Ireland, but we have had people join us from all corners of the world, too. As I write this, we have over thirty countries represented on-site this week as part of a major project. It's amazing!

I help to run all kinds of different programs depending on the group's needs. Our main aim, however, is to bring people together who wouldn't normally come together under any other circum-stances. We work on enabling relationships and trust between the groups, building bridges across the many divides that exist in our world today. I help facilitate and mediate different practical and discussion workshops, such as breaking down stereotypes, adventure learning, art therapy, identity work and team building. Corrymeela's work in Northern Ireland has shown that reconciliation is possible. Everyone is accepted for who and what they are. Corrymeela has taught us all so much, and we have all grown because of the experiences we have had here. That is the magic of Corrymeela. But as our motto goes, "Corrymeela begins when you leave!"

In Northern Ireland, there is a big divide between Protestants and Catholics. A lot of issues come down to the Catholics wanting Northern Ireland to stay part of Ireland and the Protestants wanting Ireland to stay part of Britain. The Protestants mostly refer to themselves as British, while the Catholics mostly refer to themselves as Irish. Corrymeela gives people who sometimes even come from the same town a safe environment to meet people from "the other side" and get away from the "struggles." To see them even communicating with each other is a major breakthrough. Even witnessing two young boys playing football and talking about sports together is an amazing experience, especially when you know that the religious differences between the two are so great that their only contact with each other would normally be in the form of name-calling and stones thrown across the road at one another. It makes you realize just how important the simple things are.

Because Corrymeela is a Christian community we hold worship twice a day. These worships are attended by the staff and the volunteers and anyone else who wishes to do so. Our worship sessions are somewhat different than the kind of thing most people are used to. They last about fifteen minutes and could include a poem being read, a song, an African chant, a meditation or even a game of musical chairs! Our aim is to make it an enjoyable and different experience for the groups. In the worships I lead, I like to touch on the moral side of things more than the spiritual side, as the young people who come here consider anything related to religion to be a no-go area. This is understandable when you think about the roots of all the troubles in Northern Ireland. This is where *Chicken Soup for the Teenage Soul* comes in. I use different readings from the book at different worships, and no matter what I choose to base my worship on there is always something appropriate to read. The reading that I use the most is the poem called "Please Listen." I think it is an amazing piece, and I can totally relate to it. I like to use it in the worships with young people. A lot of the youth groups that come to Corrymeela include teens who have been labeled as "problem children." Most of the time this just isn't the case. These kids have simply learned to put up walls as a defense mechanism because they are not "listened" to, and deep down they are hurting. This poem gets the listener thinking about how important it is to really be listened to and understood, and the young people can definitely relate. That is what makes Corrymeela so unique and special—we listen, and 99 percent of the time the groups come back again and keep coming back.

People of all ages have been able to relate to the readings from *Chicken Soup for the Teenage Soul*. Best of all, the pieces are written by regular people so they strike a universal chord. It is truly an inspiring book and one of the most popular ones read during worship time. It leaves the listeners with something to think about, and they often come back to worship asking, "Can you read something out of that book again?" Truly amazing. Thank you.

Peace,
Jen Ashton

Declaration of Humanhood

Dear Chicken Soup Servers,

First of all, I would like to thank you on behalf of all insecure teenagers and young adults. Your books help us understand that we are not alone. I honestly believe that the period from age ten to twenty is the most difficult and loneliest period in life. Your books are teaching us that, although we may be different on the outside, inside we're all the same. It's such a hectic time in life that we often forget we're all human. Being human we have certain rights. In order to remind myself that it's okay to be a human (and not a perfect machine), I wrote the "Declaration of Humanhood." I've sent it to you so that, if you choose to make it an ingredient in your next *Chicken Soup* book, it can remind others that they have the right to be human, too.

Declaration of Humanhood

I hereby declare that I am human.

I am human in my joy and laughter, and I am human in my pain and tears. I am human in my need to love and help others, and in my need to be loved and helped by others. I am human in my dreams and accomplishments, but most of all I am human in my flaws and mistakes.

Being human, I am entitled to the following rights:

1. I have the right to be imperfect.
2. I have the right to make many (sometimes huge) mistakes.
3. I have the right to learn from my mistakes and then move on with my life.
4. I have the right to forgive myself.
5. I have the right to feel what I feel.
6. I have the right to laugh until it hurts, and cry until it stops hurting.
7. I have the right to live my life as I choose.
8. I have the right to happiness.
9. I have the right to my own beliefs.

10. I have the right to true friends and true love.
11. I have the right to be loved by others.
12. I have the right to be loved by me.

Sincerely,
Michelle Bouchard

Misinterpreted

Although teenagers claim independence and ide-
alism, we have a common need for guidance,
love, a shoulder to occasionally cry on, and at
times a close friend to be a sounding board, to
listen without advice.

Jacqui Phillips

Dear Chicken Soup for the Teenage Soul,

The first thing I would like to say is thank you!
The stories in your books have helped me through
tough times and given me hope. Sometimes life is
so frustrating and confusing. I always thought I
was the only one who went through these hard

times and that no one else could relate to what I was going through. All teenagers are trying to unravel this tangled mess of emotions. All of us are figuring out who we are and trying to find out where we belong in the world. It's what we do in our teen years.

I hate it when I hear adults talk about how crazy teenagers are these days. The way they talk, we're all drug-using, sex-crazed, hormone-driven kids who have no goals in life. They think we're just wandering aimlessly, lost. But they have us all wrong. Most of us are scared to death because we don't know where we're going to be in ten years, or even *who* we're going to be in ten *days*. We change so fast. And we worry about so much. We worry about leaving home. We worry about college. We worry about issues like the environment and school violence. We're not who most adults think we are. We're not the "bad apples" that the media would have everyone believe we are. If they only took the time to get to know us they would see how very wrong they are.

Our days usually start with getting ready for school. No one likes to admit it, but we all wake up in the morning and try to look good. Then we're off to school. When we get there we look for our friends because we need someone to hang with. In class we work and learn, and sometimes it's hard to keep up. After school, some of us work. Some of us do activities. We go home and try to get along with our families. Then you add in taking care of yourself, having a boyfriend or girlfriend, trying to be well-liked, keeping away from drugs, homework, saying no to sex, chores, keeping out of trouble, and trying to find out who we really are. It's a lot. I get stressed out all the time, and I've only been a teenager for four months and nineteen days! I don't even have a car to worry about yet.

Thank you for writing such an awesome book for teens. I don't know what I'd do without your stories to read and fill my soul. You have put together great batches of chicken soup. Thank you again.

Yours truly,
Lizzie A. Agra

People Change but Friendships Remain

Challenge is a good thing. And in today's world, strength is an asset we have to have. Childhood, you have taught me many lessons.

Patricia Reeder

Dear Chicken Soup for the Teenage Soul,

Most people these days don't really know what a typical teenager has to go through. I don't think that anyone fully understands the pressures of being a teen and all the obstacles we overcome every day. Sure, our parents and grandparents were once teens, but things are so different now. It has never been tougher to be a teenager.

It has never been more important to be in the "right group" or to have the "right brand" of shoes. And those are the easy things to deal with. We also face problems with family, friends, relationships and school pressures. Do you remember wondering when that guy you have admired for so long would finally glance in your direction and ask you your name? Or when your parents would stop pressuring you about your grades? When it gets to be too much I turn to my friends. One friend I could not live without is *Chicken Soup for the Teenage Soul*. Your books have been so inspiring to me and have helped me to deal with and understand the problems I go through. The stories have helped me grow as a person and have truly made a big impact on my life.

I went through a confusing time with my friends when we got to junior high. I had known these friends since kindergarten, and when we began junior high it seemed like some of them began to change. We slowly drifted apart and started hanging out with different groups. When we were going through this "transition" I felt confused and hurt. It was as if we had never been friends in the first place, we had grown so far apart.

Sometime during this period I read the story "Friends Forever"* in *Chicken Soup for the Teenage*

"Friends Forever," by Phyllis Lin, Chicken Soup for the Teenage Soul II, *pp. 75–77.*

Soul II. I felt so much better after reading it. It was like a weight was lifted from me when I realized that many friendships go through changes and that we weren't the only friends to experience them. Once I understood it as a normal part of being a teenager, I started to relax and let go.

People change, but that doesn't mean we have to lose the friendships we once shared. My friends and I still spend time together when we can and care about each other a lot. Just because things are different doesn't mean that I have to forget about all the good times we had. I will always keep the memories in a safe place in my heart. This story taught me that we will go through many different changes throughout our lives. The best thing to do is to move on and let go of the past—and leave the rest in God's hands.

Sincerely,
Jiseon Choi

Giving from the Heart

Dear Chicken Soup for the Teenage Soul,

I am writing to you with heartfelt thanks for your help. In early July, I met a girl named Kristin at acting camp. As we became friends, I noticed that her life was going downhill because of her smoking, drinking and drug use.

At first I figured it would be pointless to write to people so busy and expect a response, but I figured "nothing ventured, nothing gained," and decided to write for advice anyway. You sent back a heartfelt response and three *Chicken Soup* books. Your thoughtful and generous gifts truly made a difference. The books not only helped Kristin, but rejuvenated my faith in mankind. I had noticed that the people around me were growing more and more selfish and materialistic. Your gift helped me to realize that there are still people out there willing to give from their hearts. Your act of kindness inspired me to be more dedicated than ever to helping Kristin. I gave her the books and tried to understand and sympathize with her situation.

The summer slowly slipped through our fingers, however, and on the last day of camp we found ourselves exchanging phone numbers and going our separate ways.

I started school in the fall, practiced for the school play and the soccer team, and let my hope of saving Kristin fade away. I knew that I had no control over the path she would choose to follow, and I could only wish that my prayers and caring had touched a place in her heart. As fall changed to winter, I held onto my vision of Kristin as a famous actress or photographer, happy and drug-free. The reality was probably something quite different, but I held onto my happier vision.

A few days ago, as I was cleaning my room, I came across a yellow slip of paper wedged between two books. In green ink was written Kristin's telephone number and address. I went to the phone and dialed her number with a shaky hand, thinking of what I might say. As soon as she answered, I knew things had changed.

"Kristin? It's Sarah!" I exclaimed. "How *are* you?"

She was obviously surprised and excited to hear from me, and she blurted out, "I'm drug-free!" She told me about how she was in a special drug rehabilitation school and had found new friends who supported her new attitude and healthy lifestyle.

We talked about camp, boys and Christmas gifts, and as we conversed I finally understood what people meant when they said that giving helps both the receiver *and* the giver. I felt so good in that moment that when she said "Thank you" in a very quiet and sincere way, it only made my heart expand that much more.

Thank you for teaching me about the cycle of giving: Someone gives to you, you give to someone, and that someone gives to someone else. And thanks for the stories that reassure us that loving and caring really do make a difference. I was so happy that she had found her way out of that lifestyle, and I felt so good knowing I had loved her, supported her and even, without her knowledge, prayed for her.

Sincerely,
Sarah Stillman

Moving On

I will always remember how sweet it was to love and then let go.

Rachel Obenchain

Dear Chicken Soup for the Teenage Soul,

I have enjoyed the *Teenage Soul* books from day one. They have taught me a lot and have also let me know that I am not the only one who goes through hard times, and for that I thank you. My favorite section in the books is the one on relationships. I especially have found comfort in the story "Losing the 'Us'"* about the breakup of a relationship.

---

*"Losing the 'Us'," by Lia Gay, Chicken Soup for the Teenage Soul, pp. 3–5.

I can definitely relate to that story after experiencing what I went through with my ex-boyfriend.

I can still remember the first time we met and our first few words to each other. We were sitting on a bench at a local teen hangout, and it was extremely cold, so I said aloud to anyone who cared, *"Brrr,* I'm *cold!"* No one responded so I jokingly said, "Oh well, nobody cares." Then he looked at me with his big brown eyes and said, "I care, Abbie." I was amazed that he knew my name. We started talking and ended up discussing everything and nothing that night.

A few days later, he called me and we talked as if we had been best friends for years. Then I bit the bullet and asked him if he wanted to go to a school dance that was coming up. He said yes without even hesitating. That was where we had our first kiss. I felt as if I was in heaven kissing an angel. After that, things kept getting better and better. About a week later he asked me to go steady. I told him I'd love to. From then on he completely swept me off my feet. He'd write me little love notes and give them to me between classes, or if he was walking down the hallway and saw me in a classroom, he'd call me out of class just to tell me how much I meant to him and that he loved me with all his heart.

Even though we were only together for four

months, it seemed like a lifetime. Then one Saturday morning on our four-month anniversary, I got a phone call. It was him, and he sounded so different. He told me he had fallen for someone else—his best friend. Then he told me, "There's more. Last night at a party we were talking, and we kissed." I was crushed. We both cried. Two days later we broke up and promised to be friends forever. We also promised to always care for each other. After those words we didn't speak for close to three months. I was too heartbroken to speak to him, so I asked him to give me some time.

I still love him and think of him every day, but things will never be the same. He's moved on with his life, and I'm starting to move on with mine. It was one of the hardest things I have ever had to go through. I guess we are better off as lovers that once were, than lovers that will always be.

I want to thank you and also Lia Gay because knowing I wasn't alone was a great comfort at a time when I needed it most.

Sincerely,
Abbie Stratton

Our Journey Together

Dear Chicken Soup for the Teenage Soul,

I turned twenty this summer and now I am no longer a teenager. This caused some reflection; seven years of my life, an important period, had come to an end. Most of those years were spent writing stories for the *Teenage Soul* series, and the only way to describe that experience is that it was a true blessing. It meant a lot to me as a writer, but more than that, it meant a lot to me as a person. Seeing my name in and on books was exciting, but the true joy came from all of the amazing letters I received in my four years of writing for the series.

My first semester of college was a shock. The people were different, the setting was different, and the work was (and still is) challenging. I got a C on my first college paper. Walking back to the dorm, I was disappointed in myself. I thought, *Maybe I just can't cut it as a college student. Maybe I can't cut it as a writer. Maybe I'm doomed for failure.* I returned home to my dorm and checked my mail. Inside was a letter that had been forwarded to me from the *Teenage Soul* office. It was a beautiful letter—touching and filled with gratitude. The letter was from a fifteen-year-old girl who said I had "changed her life." I realized at that moment that she would never know that, in turn, she had changed mine.

I still have that letter and many others like it. I keep them in my room and, just like letters from old friends, I take them out and read them when I'm feeling sad or just being hard on myself. That is what is wonderful about what I get to do. A community of teens has been built around these books, and it's not only the writers giving to the readers; it's everyone helping each other. Reading and writing for these books have changed my life. The readers have changed my life, and the other writers who give of themselves, their fears and their dreams have changed me, too.

I try to respond to all of the letters I receive but, I must admit, there are times when I have neglected to do so. I apologize to those of you whom I have not responded to, but it is very important to me to still be an active part of this loving community. I feel blessed to say that I am part of a community of people who really want to learn about themselves and understand others. Some of them have the courage to say, "I need some help," and some of them have the strength to write about it. Thank you for all of your wonderful letters and thank you for taking that journey through being a teen with me. I know now that I was never really alone because, through reading your letters, I realize we were and are all going through it together.

I used to say, "I can't wait until I'm not a teenager anymore." Now that I'm not, I find myself missing it. Strange how that works. Those seven years held some of the most important decisions and learning experiences of my life. So I made myself a promise to try not to forget those feelings, ever, so that maybe someday we will all be understood.

Dream big dreams!

With my sincerest gratitude,

Lia Gay

If They Can Make It, So Can I

So the world just keeps on turning. One personal event does not make the difference in the Earth's rotation. It makes the difference in the life and heart of the people involved, which makes love one of the most worthwhile, cherished, tingly, confusing, valuable, but vital feelings in the world.

Joanna Taylor

Dear Chicken Soup,

I'm in my senior year of high school and next year I'll be going off to college. This has been a particularly difficult year for me in anticipation of my transition from high school to college. My friend introduced me to *Chicken Soup for the Teenage Soul* and quite honestly it has helped me in so many ways.

I usually read thrillers and mystery novels, but once I picked up this book and read it, I couldn't put it down until I had read it entirely. I literally sat on my bed and cried for hours, realizing that I wasn't alone and that there are people out there who are just like me. With this book you feel the greatest gift of all—love. You feel it in the stories you read and in the realization that there are people out there for you. Sometimes you just aren't looking in the right direction.

Right after I read it, I got the courage to tell my best friend that I loved him and that I would miss him when we go our separate ways. I let down my guard and told my little sister that I loved her even though it has been very hard for us to get along. I also began to treat my friends and even acquaintances how any person should be treated—with respect and kindness, just like I would expect from them. I realized that sometimes people have hard times and that first impressions aren't always the truth. I learned that even though people are different, that doesn't make them strange. It makes them brave, strong and interesting.

Just recently I was accepted to Oregon State University. So many emotions rushed through me, but the one that hit the hardest was sadness. I would have to leave someone that I hold very dear to me—my best friend. Even though we have only become close in the last seven months, I have a connection with him that I haven't had with anyone else. When I read "First Love,"* by Mary Ellen Klee, I cried until I had gotten it all out. Over the past few months I have been worrying more and more about leaving and losing touch with him and not realizing what a great time I could be having with him now, before I leave. I know that even though our lives' paths may separate us for the time being, we will never lose each other. Thank you for saving me from heartache.

I hold this book close to my heart. Even though I must return it to my friend tomorrow, I will still have the stories in my heart. Whenever something makes me stumble in life, I will remember all the strong and courageous people in the stories and know that if they can make it, then so can I.

Sincerely,
Kristen Morris

---

*"First Love," by Mary Ellen Klee, Chicken Soup for the Teenage Soul, pp. 28–30.

A Closer Family

Nothing can make everything okay after a hard experience, but the simple act of giving a hug can come pretty close.

Hannah Boyd

Dear Chicken Soup for the Teenage Soul,

I am writing to thank you for the story "Healing with Love"* by Cecile Wood in your new edition of *Chicken Soup for the Teenage Soul III.* As soon as I started reading the first line and the words "reform school" leaped off the page, I knew I was going to be able to relate to the story.

———

*"Healing with Love," by Cecile Wood, Chicken Soup for the Teenage Soul III, *pp. 108–111.*

My brother was dealing with a drug problem last year and had to be checked in to a center for kids with drug problems. He was eighteen at the time. Being at the center made him a whole new person. Before he went, we couldn't even speak to him. We would ask him how his day went, and he would respond with only a nod. He never even said "Hi" or "Bye" to us. We felt completely shut out of his life.

He was allowed no family contact at all for the first three weeks of the program. After the three weeks were over, my whole family went to visit him. He was waiting for us outside and greeted us all with big hugs. I was shocked and didn't hide it. I asked him what they had done to him, and he told me that he had just "grown up."

That entire day he couldn't stop talking about how much he enjoyed being there and thanking my parents for having sent him there. I was so happy for him. It felt like I finally had my brother back.

In the story in the book, Cecile wrote about not being able to have a meal at the center where she was visiting her brother without crying. I had the same experience. When I had lunch with my brother and the other residents later that day, it was a struggle for me to hold back my tears. It was sad to look at the kids working so hard to get themselves together and pull themselves back up. I wondered what had brought each of them down so low to begin with.

Not all of the kids were alone that weekend; there were some other parents there, too. Everyone seemed genuinely happy and proud of their sons or daughters. There were a lot of tears shed.

My brother and I were closer after that weekend. We would talk on the phone all the time. He called me once a week, and we would talk for hours and hours. I guess we had a lot of catching up to do.

He's nineteen now, and he just finished his treatment program. He's been sober and off drugs for almost an entire year now. I'm so happy for him, and my family feels closer than we've ever been. Yesterday I made my brother read the story "Healing with Love." He read it out loud in front of my parents and my twenty-two-year-old brother. He couldn't finish it because he started crying halfway through. I guess it was difficult to remember all the pain he had to go through to get to where he is today. I finished the story for him. My whole family could relate, and it made us all feel so grateful that my brother was able to "heal with love." Thank you again for this wonderful story of hope and healing.

Sincerely,
Lissa Desjardins

Dealing with My Mother's Death

Dear Teenage Chicken Soup,

Thank you for the uplifting stories that you have published. I own two inspirational books, *Chicken Soup for the Teenage Soul* and *Chicken Soup for the Christian Soul*. The stories in both books are filled with what this world should be more like.

I used to be a drug and alcohol abuser at the age of thirteen. I felt invincible, and I rebelled. I didn't understand the method of discipline my parents used at that time. They believed that if you misbehaved, you should pay the consequences for your actions. Some months down the road a tragedy struck our household. My mother, who was suffering from congestive heart failure, passed away. I felt cut off from the world and that God had turned his back on me. My friends helped me relieve the pain, but it would come back like a wave washing over me. All I had to do was look around at home. It was a constant reminder. It was so bad that I ended up staying at a friend's house for close to six months. I was always able to cover up the pain with distractions that would seem to keep my mind off her. I knew deep down inside at some point I would have to deal with my real feelings and emotions surrounding my mother's death. That time came very recently.

It started out as a normal day, until I turned on the radio. "Amazing Grace" blared into my ears. It was the song sung at my mother's funeral. I instantly broke down. At first, I began blaming my mom, then myself, then God. The barricades blocking my memory broke down and I had to finally face that my mother was no longer here. She was never going to return and there was nothing I could do about it. I cried, then prayed, then cried some more. I couldn't take it. It wasn't fair. Everyone else I knew had mommies. I didn't want to be different in that aspect of my life. Yet, the harsh fact still remains: I am motherless. It still hurts to look back on those memories, but it made me who am I today. Her golden smile is my favorite memory of her, and I know she is keeping heaven radiant with that same smile.

The books you have written are truly special. I

would like to tell you from the bottom of my heart, THANK YOU!!!! This world is full of tragedy, disaster, fear, hatred, anger and remorse. The books you have published have shown me that this world is also full of goodness.

Love,
Amanda L. Poff

A Buoy in the Ocean of Life

Dear Chicken Soup for the Teenage Soul,

In January 1996, the year I started high school, my father committed suicide. For two years, I held everything inside, never letting out how much I missed my dad. It was so painful to know that my dad and I would never spend those special times together. He'd never be able to see his "Little Pooh Bear" walk into high school on her first day or see her win a first-place trophy on her new horse.

Over the next two years I became progressively more depressed and withdrawn. I was miserable and could not remember what it felt like to be happy. All I felt was sadness and the overwhelming sense of having been rejected.

In 1998, I was put on medication and started counseling. I was told that I should be in therapy and on the pills for six months. After six months, I was still feeling physically and emotionally exhausted. I tried to stop taking my medication, but every time I did, I just collapsed back into my sinkhole. That was when I first heard of your books.

My mom gave me the first *Chicken Soup for the Teenage Soul* for my birthday. I could not put it down. It helped me gain a more positive attitude once again. I felt as if I could overcome my despair, and I started thinking toward the future again. Eventually I started feeling strong enough to get off my medication and stop therapy. After a year of being helped, I was ready to help myself.

It is now January 2000, and in three days it will be the anniversary of my dad's death. It has been four long, hard years, but with the help of family, friends and, of course, *Chicken Soup*, I've managed to experience gratitude for all of my hardships and times of trial. I believe that I have grown tremendously in mind and spirit by living through these tough experiences.

I recently received *Chicken Soup for the Teenage Soul II*, and it is helping me deal with my mom's new marriage and my new stepfamily. I would like to thank you for these books. I'm sure that teenagers all over the world feel the same way that I do. These books are a lifesaver, a buoy to hold onto in the ocean of life. I am truly grateful to you all for all of the hard work you put into these books. Your work is *greatly* appreciated. Thank you.

Yours sincerely,

Kirett Kay

[*Editors' note:* Depression is a serious illness and often requires therapy and medication. While many people have found comfort and support within the pages of *Chicken Soup* books, we encourage those in need of further help to seek professional guidance and medical advice as needed.]

Feeling Better About Myself

Dear Chicken Soup Folks,

My name is Adam. I'm now a sophomore at the University of Illinois, Champaign/Urbana. I just want to say thanks for putting together such a great series of books. I have a disease called alopecia areata, which is a condition that results in the loss of hair on the scalp and elsewhere. It occurs in males and females of all ages, but young persons are affected the most. It has come up four times in my life: first in fourth grade, then sixth grade, then it appeared again during my sophomore year of high school. Being so young in grade school, I never thought much of it, but I was quite a bit more sensitive to it in high school, so I went to see a doctor. I had never heard of anyone having anything like this, and it was really hard. I ended up shaving off the rest of my hair my senior year. I only had about a third of it left anyway. It was a difficult thing to explain to people.

A year or two after I was diagnosed, I came across the wonderful story, "No-Hair Day,"* in *Chicken Soup for the Teenage Soul* about a girl who had alopecia. I can't tell you how much of a comfort that story has been to me. After I read that, I couldn't let myself get down about it anymore. I'm still bald, although I had a full head of hair for about six months earlier this year. I still struggle with feeling unattractive and self-conscious. But that story has given me a great example of someone who dealt with her hair loss, and people's reaction to it, in a positive way. Thank you very much, and keep up the good work.

Sincerely,
Adam Heise

---

* *"No-Hair Day," by Jennifer Rosenfeld and Alison Lambert,* Chicken Soup for the Teenage Soul, *pp. 325–327.*

Me

Dear Chicken Soup for the Teenage Soul,

I have been an ardent fan of the *Chicken Soup for the Soul* series for a while now. The first *Chicken Soup* book I ever read was from my English teacher's personal library. As soon as I started reading it I found myself getting addicted to it. I could relate to most of the stories in it, and I realized that there are people out there going through the same things that I was (even though the stories took place in America). It did not matter what country they were from; similar situations happen all around the globe. I was not alone.

One of the messages I picked up from story after story was that attitude plays such an important part in the outcome of situations. I decided that I would try to look at the positive side of things, and this has really helped me to be a happier person. The other thing I learned was the importance of writing as a tool for overcoming depression. When I am feeling down I will get out my pen and jot down all my negative feelings. This really helps me.

I also love to write poetry. I have sent you a poem as a thank-you for the books and the inspiration.

Sincerely,
Wanda Marie Goh Jen Jen
Malaysia

Me

Swirls of color, fabric of silk,

Breakfast as simple as cornflakes and milk.

Occult fascinates and horror chills,

Just a teenager finding some thrills.

Beaches of white, oceans of blue,

The love of my life and it is true.

Nature and music entwine as one,

Homework and papers and books never done.

Friends misunderstand; that is what I can't stand.

Why don't they take me as I am?

I rebel but with a cause,

To change all within me that is flawed.

Understand me; it's not very hard,

Emotions play a very big part.

Thoughts of mine fly like colors in time,

Sing songs of harmony that fall in rhyme.

Try to understand me is all I ask,

Try to understand me and this, too, shall pass.

Wanda Marie Goh Jen Jen

4

INSIGHTS
AND LESSONS

Life is a succession of lessons which must be lived to be understood.

Thomas Carlyle

Bonding with Notebooks

Today could be the day that my mom real-
izes I'm growing up and gives me some more
responsibility.

Jenny Gleason

Dear Chicken Soup for the Teenage Soul,

I have always been a real fan of your books and the important lessons of love and understanding that are shared in each of the stories. They have helped me to see things that were not so clear to me. I have received a great deal of comfort from reading many of the stories.

I had been going through some difficult times not so long ago dealing with the pressures of growing up and trying to communicate with my parents, particularly my mother. Our relationship had suffered because of this. When I would get frustrated or angry it seemed like we would end up in some sort of confrontation with each other and not talk about what we were really feeling. I feel like I have overcome those obstacles now, but not without a certain turn of events.

A while back I ran away from home so that I could be far enough away to vent my anger and release some of the pain bottled up inside of me. I stayed away for many hours, well into the night, before I finally decided to return home. When I walked through the front door of my house, I immediately saw all the pain, anger and disappointment on my parents' faces, especially my mother's. For days after the incident, my mom and I were on unfirm ground, to say the least. Everything we did or said was filled with tension until we both eventually snapped. We knew we desperately had to have a talk. We agreed to have breakfast together the next morning. That morning will remain etched in my memory forever. It was a turning point in both of our lives and our relationship.

We decided to go to a local café. On our way to the table I noticed that my mother had two notebooks and some pens. I asked her what they were for. She explained to me that sometimes it is easier to write down our feelings rather than try to talk about them. She then proceeded to hand me a notebook of my own and she kept one for herself. The "rules" for that talk were that she would pick a topic, and we would write down our feelings about the topic in the form of a letter. It could be as long or as short as we wanted. Our first topic was: "Why I am so angry." I had written a half page worth of stuff, and my mom filled up nearly three pages. I watched tears stream down her face as she wrote. I never realized anyone could hide so much anger and frustration. It could have been that I never paid much attention, either. Sometimes we think we are the only ones with problems, but I was reminded that morning that other people can be hurting just as much.

After she was finished writing we exchanged our notebooks and read what the other had written. As soon as I started reading my mother's words, I began to cry and so did she. When we were finished reading we discussed our feelings. Amazingly enough, it felt like all the anger I had welled up inside of me drained from my body. Our talk helped me realize so many things I had never thought of before, not only about my mother but about other people as well.

My mother and I continue to use our notebooks as a means of communicating our anger and frustrations, and our happiness also. We know that no matter how we feel about each other, our notebooks are a safe place to express it. We have made a pact that at the end of each letter we write, "I love you." Here are two of our more recent entries:

Dear Mom,

I just wanted you to know that some things I do are not meant to hurt or spite you. When I yell at you it's not because I hate you. And when I tell you I hate you, you should know that I really don't, although at times I feel like you hate me. Sometimes you just make me really mad and frustrated, and I don't know what to do with it. Like when you tell me you don't believe me even though I'm not lying, or when you do things that invade my privacy without my permission that you know I won't like. For instance, the other day you searched my room without me knowing or being there. I just wanted to hate you so much then. Then today you yelled at me, and it made me so mad. I really don't think there is much more to say right now. I love you.

Katte

And my mother's response to my letter:

Dear Katie,

I realize that you get mad and frustrated, but I do, too. I don't want you to think that since I am an adult I don't have feelings. As much as you think that I might like it, I don't like yelling at you. I just wish you would help out a little more with the family and around the house. It would make things easier on me. Some things I do, like searching your room or not believing you, are not done to be mean. I only do those things if I have good cause. Sometimes you worry me, but it's just because I care. Although you might not think so, you yell at me as much as I yell at you. It hurts my feelings as well. Sometimes I just want to cry. I'm glad you told me how you felt about all those things. I'll try to work on my temper with you, and I'll try to be more patient if you will return the same courtesy to me and help me out a little around the house. If this is not okay, tell me and we can try to work something out. I love you.

Mom

We gained a special gift that day at the restaurant and we continue to be blessed with each other's everlasting love and patience. I am now a firm believer that we all need to express our feelings in order to live healthy lives. Thank you so much for letting me share this with you.

Sincerely,
Katie Benson

Life Is a Bumpy Road

Dear Kimberly,

Chicken Soup for the Teenage Soul was such a blessing for me. The quotes and stories really opened my eyes to all new perspectives in life. I am only twenty-three, and I have been incarcerated for seven years. This book has given me the courage to share my story with you.

When I was sixteen, I had my mind set on two things: having fun and being cool. One Saturday night, a friend and I knocked off from work at a local grocery store and could think of nothing better to do than ride around and get drunk. I never expected how drastically my life would change before that night ended.

After I was intoxicated, I came up with the "coolest" idea to show off in front of my older friend. "Hey man, let's go get my gun and find someone to scare by shooting at them." My friend didn't see anything wrong with the idea, so we went and got the gun. The alcohol, and now the gun, gave me all the "courage" I needed to show off. We finally passed a boy walking by himself along the road, and I just pointed the gun out of the window and started firing. He was fatally wounded and died right there on the side of the road.

I have now been paying for those actions for the past seven years as I sit in the Louisiana State Penitentiary serving a mandatory life sentence without parole. Like a lot of teens, I never worried about the consequences of my actions. I didn't care what happened tomorrow. I just wanted to have all the "fun" I could have today, but there was a price to pay. I'm afraid too many of us are making foolish decisions that come at such a high price, and we will never be able to clear ourselves of the consequences.

I am often asked what's the most important lesson I've learned, or what would I tell teens if I could only say one thing to them. It would be this: Life is a bumpy road with many regrets and very few second chances, so think before you act.

I have missed a lot of things in life. But reading all the stories in *Chicken Soup for the Teenage Soul* has taught me many things. I am thankful for the wonderful work y'all have done. Please keep up the awesome job. I can hardly wait for the new one to come out.

Thankfully yours,
Gary LeRoux

Learning the Hard Way

Dear Chicken Soup for the Teenage Soul,

My name is Kim, and I am from Ohio. I have really enjoyed reading your books. My friend Chelsea introduced me to them, and I've been reading them ever since.

I am fifteen years old—and five months pregnant. One subject I haven't read much about in your books is that of teenage pregnancy and its consequences. Girls and guys my age do not realize how serious it is to have sex. My mom always tried to warn me about making better choices for myself. She warned me about the serious things that could happen to me like getting pregnant, and contracting an STD or AIDS. But I never listened.

I've made a lot of mistakes. And now I'm

pregnant. The father is not going to be in my life—
or the baby's life, for that matter. I would give anything to be able to take it all back, but I can't. My
only hope is that I can help to prevent it from happening to someone else by sharing with teens the
extent of my remorse.

The stories in the book *have* helped me to do the
right thing in other areas of my life. Last weekend
my friends who had been drinking told me they
would take me home. But having read the story
about a guy who was killed when he let his friends
drive drunk, I decided to call my mom and ask her
to pick me up. My friends didn't think I was a dork
or anything, because I was just looking out for
myself and my baby. I felt very positive about my
decision. My mom was proud of me, too.

I hope your books continue to teach us lessons
and open our eyes. It's hard to listen to our parents
all the time. Sometimes it helps to be able to take
our life lessons in the form of a story, rather than
the bitter medicine of our parents' lectures. Thank
you.

Sincerely,
Kim Lowery

My Magic Mirror

Dear Chicken Soup,

I haven't been as fortunate or as lucky as my friends when it comes to dating and relationships. Everyone else always seems to be able to "get the guy." One Friday night I was sitting at home without a date while all my friends were out with their boyfriends and I was inspired to write this poem:

My Magic Mirror

There is a mirror in my house,
It's on my bathroom wall.
Although I've met some other ones,
It's the friendliest of all.

It doesn't matter when I look,
It can happen any time.
A beautiful reflection it will show,
And then I'll see it's mine.

So how does it make me look so good,
At any time of day?
And why can't all the guys at school,
See me in my mirror's way?

If they could only see that girl,
Who greets me with a smile,
Then maybe I'd have a date, or two—
Hasn't happened in a while.

But do I want to date a guy,
Who'll judge by what he sees?
Or do I want to date a guy
Who will love and appreciate me?

He'll love me for my intelligence,
My humor and my taste.
He'll love me for my selflessness,
Which I haven't put to waste.

He'll love me for the things I do,
And how I get them done.

He'll love me with each breath I take,
And with each ray of the sun.

So then when will he find me,
And in my mirror see?
When will he come to fill the void,
That aches inside of me?

Will he show up on my front door,
When I'm about to give up hope?
Or will he come when I'm at peace within,
With the strength inside to help me cope?

Because I'm not just what's on the outside,
I am me down to my core.
And as I learn to love myself,
There will be a guy who loves me more.

A week later, I met a guy who I really liked. Unfortunately, that didn't work out, but I was okay with that because I believe in what my poem says about a guy loving you for *you*.

Since then, it's been like a lucky charm. Now that I finally allowed myself to have that kind of confidence, my teenage years are looking much better! I never used to believe it when teenage magazines would say that as soon as you have confidence, guys would pick up on it and take interest. After experiencing this for myself, however, I want to let everyone else know that it does work.

I hope my poem can help at least one person in the same way your books have helped me. So, for all those teenagers sitting at home on a Friday night: Stop waiting around, throw on a smile and lift your chin high!

Thank you,
Melinda Allen

It's Not What's on the Outside, but What's on the Inside

Dear Chicken Soup for the Teenage Soul,

I am writing to thank you for teaching me what to value in other people. Your books have taught me that it is a person's character and what's in a person's heart that matter the most—not what people look like or the clothes they wear.

Recently I fell hard for a guy at our school. His name is Nick. The first time I laid eyes on him I thought I had come face-to-face with an angel. He was absolutely the most beautiful human being I had ever encountered. When he walked down the hallways at school, every female within a six-foot radius would turn and follow him with their gaze. He was tall, dark and handsome—a regular Prince Charming. His eyes were a deep chestnut brown, and when directed toward me could send shivers down my spine and turn my knees to gelatin. Upon pointing him out to my closest friend, the obvious thing happened: She, too, fell head-over-heels for Nick.

The two of us followed him around school so often he could have pressed charges against us for harassment. We sent him countless love letters and verses of bad poetry. Every day after school, we lingered by his car, waited for him to get in it and then watched him wistfully as he drove away. We were under his spell, and we had become stalkers.

As time passed, however, I noticed that even though Nick had a shiny, beautiful exterior, his interior needed a little work. His personality struck me as icy and self-centered. Following him so closely all the time gave me the chance to hear the rude comments he made to people, and it shattered my fantasy. My Prince Charming was turning out to be not so charming after all!

Eventually reality sunk in. Yes, Nick was beautiful on the outside, but inside he was made of stone. And even though I realized my knight-in-shining-armor was a fraud, I was not brokenhearted. Instead, I was grateful to him for showing me that I truly do care about more than superficial appearances. I now know that true beauty comes from the heart—not the face. Your books have reinforced that for me. Thank you for sharing these stories with us teens. Maybe one day even the Nicks of the world will read them and learn a thing or two about kindness and character.

Sincerely,
Caitlin Pollock

A Simple Story

Dear Chicken Soup for the Teenage Soul,

When my story "Choices"* was published in *Chicken Soup for the Teenage Soul II*, I never imagined I would receive so many letters from teens dealing with a similar situation. It is funny, but at the time I felt like I was the only one dealing with changes in friendship. I have come to realize that everybody has a time when things start to change, and people who you were once close to slowly drift away. Accepting this can be difficult and can leave you feeling so alone. I have heard from so many teens from all over the world (yes, the world!) who have been through these changes, or are experiencing them right now. It is so wonderful

---

*"Choices," by Alicia M. Boxler, Chicken Soup for the Teenage Soul II, pp. 71–73.

to know that a simple *Chicken Soup* story could inspire them to write and share their story with me.

As I said, I have received hundreds of letters from teenagers from places such as India and Indonesia, to South Carolina and Canada. Each letter touches my heart so much and each one makes me realize how grateful I am that I was able to share my stories with others. I am glad that so many people could relate to what I was going through; almost every letter includes something about how my story was real to their life also.

"When I read your story, it touched my heart. I guess it is because I can completely relate to it!" Carlise

"I really like your story. I was in the same situation as you were with one of my friends." Jessica

One of the most popular questions I get asked is how a story gets chosen to be included in a *Chicken Soup* book. The only answer I have is to write something that people can relate to, tell a story that when the reader is finished, he or she sits back and says, "That sounds like they were writing about my life."

Though I read every letter, it is hard finding the time to keep in touch with every person who writes me. Everyone has his or her own story to tell, and the lessons I have learned have outnumbered the ones I will ever teach. I have read letters from teens crying out for help, and others willing to offer advice. The most important lesson I have learned is the value of sharing your experiences with others. Each of us has obstacles that we have to deal with, and we must learn how to overcome them.

I treasure the letters I receive. These teens have become more than just pen pals, they have become my friends. Their personal stories have made me realize how precious friendship is. Throughout your life people will drift away, but many new people will come into your heart and they will stay. This is my inspiration. Thank you for giving it to me. The following is a sampling of the letters I have received that affected me greatly.

Sincerely,
Alicia M. Boxler

Alicia,

My name is Carlise Richards. I read your story entitled "Choices" from <u>Chicken Soup for the Teenage Soul II</u>. When I read your story it touched my heart. I guess it is because I can completely relate to it! My friend, Maria, and I are separating mainly because of her boyfriend, Ivan. I know it's strange for me to open myself up like this, but I feel like you are the only person who can understand.

I guess in a way I'm jealous that she has someone and I don't. All the time that was spent talking and bonding is gone. I mean once in a while we'll go shopping or have a cappuccino, but when we do, it is all about Ivan. I do have other friends, and I started going to my church's youth group, but that doesn't replace my best friend. I am a senior, and Maria is a sophomore. I don't mean to sound selfish, but this year was supposed to be full of fun, friends and memories. So far it's been memories. When I leave for college, I don't want it to be on bad terms. At night, I lay in my bed and think that if I had a boyfriend in my life, I wouldn't be so lonely. I realize that it is not going to solve anything. Maria has to realize that boys come and go, but friends will always be there. I will always be there for her, but who's going to be there for me? I'm glad that she is happy. I just feel like I lost my best friend. I just thought that I would write to say that your story touched me and share my experiences.

Sincerely,
Carlise Michelle Richards

Lessons

I've learned that the greatest achievements aren't always awards or prizes. My greatest achievement is nothing material; it is the valuable lesson I learned about the human spirit. Awards fade away, prizes lose their luster, but lessons learned are lessons forever.

Leslie Herrel

Dear Chicken Soup for the Soul,

Few books make you look into your soul. Your books do just that. They make you evaluate what kind of person you are. Are you the type of person who harasses people who seem different from you or are you the type who sees good in others?

My life was never perfect. I was not the most popular person around, and I was often made fun of by other students. I have many mental scars that I will never forget. I hated those kids who picked on me, and I vowed that I would never forgive them. I now wish I had lived by the golden rule: *Do unto others what you would have them do to you.* I did not. Instead, I picked on other people less fortunate than myself. I remember one boy in grade school who was poor, overweight and had a speech impediment. The kids in my class used to pick on him constantly. Later, in high school, I realized what I had done, and I could not forgive myself. I wished I had stood up for this person, but I couldn't go back and change what I had done, though I wanted to.

I love your books for the lessons they teach. I have learned so much from them. They have taught me about compassion, something I seem to lack. They have shown me what it means to love, to live and to experience true sadness. I have learned that everyone is special, and that we all have our own talents. The stories on suicide showed me that no matter how bad things seem, it is not worth taking your own life. I, too, have people who love me and who would truly miss me.

I realized that my parents have experienced what I am going through, and they have seen the same things that I have seen. They do know what is best for me. Most of all, I learned that I can't be perfect, and that no one is. Those boys who picked on me, I now forgive. I know now that people change and we all grow. Though they hurt me very much, I can say that I forgive them. I hope the boy I picked on in grade school has grown to forgive me.

Your books are about others' joys and failures. They are about learning and growing from one's mistakes. I want you to know that I have become a better person because of the lessons in your books.

Sincerely,
Michele Fiorentini

Wiping Off the Fog

Dear Chicken Soup for the Teenage Soul,

One night I was sitting in my bathtub reading *Chicken Soup for the Teenage Soul II*. I was reading the section on friendship and one of the stories about friends and family and how they all pull together in times of crisis. For some reason, this story really hit me. As I was getting out of the bathtub I noticed that the pictures on the wall were all fogged over from the intense heat of the water. That was when I realized that I had been fogging up my life, trying to cover everything up.

There were a lot of things going wrong in my family and life. My parents had just finalized their divorce, and my mom (who I live with) was a wreck and always sad and crying. This kind of made me embarrassed as a thirteen-year-old with a mother crying in public. So I did what I thought a normal person should do: I covered it up to make it look like nothing was happening. My mom's mom and my dad's dad were both suffering from cancer. My mom had already lost her dad to cancer when she was only twelve. My mom was having such a hard time having to go through it all over again with her mom.

At school you couldn't tell that anything was wrong with me, until one day when I just started crying in the middle of class. The teacher knew right away that I needed somebody to talk to. He let one of my good friends and me go out in the hall to talk. We sat there and cried for a while until we convinced each other we could get through this together. (She, too, was having lots of problems.)

When I am at home I don't know what to do. I have a lot of friends, and I want to get out of the house because the surroundings just aren't stable for me there, but I also want to stay with my mom to let her know I am there for her. I really don't like to get into that kind of mushy stuff, though. Whenever my mom is crying I usually let my sister sit with her and try to comfort her.

It was then, that night in the bathroom, as I was wiping the fog off the pictures, that I realized I should be doing the same thing in my life. I should let all my steam off by telling people how I feel. I need to wipe away all of the fog in my life and try to be with my family, especially in this time of crisis. Your book helped me understand this.

Sincerely,
Katie Ecker

The Soft Voice of Forgiveness

As the feeling of betrayal is the worst feeling ever for me, forgiveness is probably the best.

Rae B. Ramos

Dear Chicken Soup for the Teenage Soul,

We hear so many negative things about teenagers and certainly some episodes concern us all. But we need to be sure to spread the good news, too, and I feel the following is indeed good news.

As a vice principal of a high school for many years, I was a pretty good judge of character and nothing surprised me. That was until I got to know a soft-spoken teenager named Stephanie. She entered my office in tears one day when her wallet had been stolen out of her backpack during chemistry class. Her classmates had seen another student, Dustin, take her wallet and escape to a nearby restroom. By the time her friends could alert campus security, twenty-three dollars had been taken from her wallet.

When I summoned Dustin to my office, he admitted taking the wallet to the restroom and looking in it. He would not, however, confess to taking the money even though the empty wallet was found in the restroom. I told him that since he took the wallet, he was now responsible for replacing its contents. He had one week to bring the money, or I would suspend him for stealing which, as a violation of the school athletic code, would also mean he would be off the track team.

I tried to call Dustin's father all that afternoon, but the phone was always busy. Finally at 7:00 P.M., I managed to contact him and told him of the incident. He assured me that Dustin would return the money.

A week flew by, and Stephanie stood meekly in my doorway once more. With downcast eyes and a sad smile on her face, she said that Dustin had not yet returned the money. I tried Dustin's father's work number again and this time was able to get through right away. What a shock it was for me to hear a different voice. He was clearly not the person I had talked to the week before. I quickly explained the theft of the wallet, telling him that I had given Dustin a chance to save face by returning the money. Dustin had not only ignored the opportunity, but had compounded his error by impersonating his father on the phone and withholding the truth from him. Dustin's father said that he didn't take this lightly and insisted on bringing Dustin in personally, after his suspension was over, to meet with Stephanie and me.

During the conference, while we waited for Stephanie to come to my office, Dustin's father filled me in on some background. Up until two years before, Dustin had lived with his mother in Los Angeles until she could no longer deal with his rebellious nature. He had come to Sacramento to live with his father who was much more of a disciplinarian. Dustin was having a difficult time making the adjustment, as was his father, a single, working parent. His father appreciated my willingness to work with Dustin, rather than merely dole out punishment, as was done in the Washington, D.C., high school he himself had attended as a teenager. He confided that if he had done what Dustin had, he would have been sent to juvenile hall and immediately locked up.

When Stephanie arrived, Dustin squirmed in his chair and crossed his arms. His father introduced himself to Stephanie and apologized to her on Dustin's behalf. Dustin kept his face blank, staring at a picture on my wall. After a long pause, his father prompted him to speak to her. "Dustin, don't you have something to say?" Dustin shrugged his shoulders but stayed put, glaring at his father whose eyes had suddenly narrowed. Through clenched teeth, he said, "Say it, Dustin. Now!" Walking over to Stephanie, Dustin reluctantly handed her a closed envelope and begrudgingly muttered, "I'm sorry I took your wallet. Here's your money." Stephanie looked at him with wide brown eyes and gently said, "I forgive you."

Stunned, Dustin stared at her in disbelief. He blinked his eyes and grimaced, as if the spotlight had suddenly been turned on him.

After both students had returned to class, Dustin's father stayed to talk to me. He shared with me that he had recently taken Dustin to a therapist to begin working on the root of his behavioral problems. Some trauma had happened to Dustin around the age of eight, and, now that it had been uncovered, counseling might help him get rid of his self-destructive tendencies and improve his self-esteem. I told him that I was glad to hear he was seeking professional help for his son and promised to keep in touch with him if any more problems arose. They never did.

Dustin stayed on the track team, went on to excel academically and was never referred to this office again. Through ongoing counseling, he was eventually able to accept and even like himself. Stephanie had shown him the way. By forgiving him, she taught him how to forgive himself. I often think of Stephanie because, on the surface, she looked like a fragile flower that might drop its petals at the slightest breeze. But she had me fooled. Inside, where it really counts, she was invincible, using her wisdom, power and courage to help a classmate who needed to turn his life around. Laurence Sterne once wrote: "Only the brave know how to forgive." Meek and soft-spoken Stephanie turned out to be the bravest one of all.

Thanks so much,

Jennifer Martin

5

TOUGH STUFF

It is only when we are deeply suffering that
we earnestly seek what is true and essential.
Pain humbles us in the best way.

Kimberly Kirberger

Honoring My Sister

Dear Ms. Kirberger,
Mr. Canfield and Mr. Hansen,

I am enclosing a piece of writing that I wrote last year as a senior in high school. It describes my experiences regarding the death of my sister, Susan. Susan was in a car accident when she was sixteen and lived in a vegetative state until she finally died two years later. Her vibrant life and prolonged death have been the most influential events of my life, as they forced me to question so many things about the way I was living.

I truly hope that you will consider this piece for publication in your next edition of *Chicken Soup for the Teenage Soul*. I would love to share the story of Susan's life and the dramatic impact that it had on me as her little sister. I wrote this piece many years after her death, and it therefore reflects the long healing process that has consumed me for so many years. I will never get over her death, and in fact, the injustice of a promising life taken so young still gives me chills. I have, however, come to the point where I no longer feel sadness and anger when I think about her, but rather a sense of peace and happiness. It is important for me to be able to share with your readers that it is possible to return to happiness while still honoring the memory of your lost loved one. This is the main purpose of my essay. Thank you for your time and consideration.

Sincerely,

Laura Glenn Thornhill

A Lesson in Beauty

I sit at my desk, my body hunched over the keyboard, and I try to write. My eyes are tired from staring at the blank computer screen, and the muscles in my neck throb from hours of such poor posture. It is 1:00 A.M., and my literary analysis is due in eight hours. I frantically try to write an introduction, but nothing that comes to my mind seems good enough. As my eyes wander away from the computer, my

thoughts drift to the soft flannel sheets and feather pil-
lows that beckon me from just four feet away. It seems
my entire week has been stressful, staying up late to
finish assignments and then going to school early to
work in the yearbook lab. Again, my eyes drift away
from the screen, but this time they catch a glimpse of
a miniature tea set that sits on a shelf above my computer. My eyes focus on the tiny tea set, and I pick it
up, holding it all together at first, and then piece by
piece. It is white with a blue Oriental pattern, and the
pieces are rimmed with strips of gold. On some of
the saucers the tiny pattern is crooked, and on the
pitcher, the gold stripe is uneven, and the design runs
off the edge. It has been seven years since I eagerly
unwrapped the silver paper and first held this tea set
in the palm of my hand. My eyes well up with tears,
and I remember.

It is Christmas Eve. I am ten years old. Posed
together for a family photo, I stand in the center of my
sisters and cousins on the elegant stairway in our
foyer. My eyes are distracted by two Christmas trees
shining across the room, both glowing with lights and
glass ornaments. On the top of one perches a shiny
gold star, and from my place on the stairs, I can see

the entire room by looking into its reflection. "Laura, keep your eyes on the camera," my aunt says, "I just want to take a few more pictures." I try to stay still as we endure the awkwardness of posing for yet another photograph. After the camera flashes, I look at the star again, and in its reflection, I can see my sister Susan standing behind me. As usual, Susan is smiling, and in her flowing black dress, she stands out from all of us. Her thick, corkscrew curls cascade down her shoulders, and her chestnut eyes glitter with excitement. I am in complete awe of my beautiful sister, so I try to imitate her radiant smile for the next photo.

According to our family tradition, each child is to open a present on Christmas Eve. I walk around the tree, carefully inspecting every present addressed to me. I want to save all of the bigger ones for the morning, so I choose to open a small box beautifully wrapped in silver paper. "Laura, that present is from me," says Susan. "I wouldn't open it now if I were you, because you might be disappointed." "I'm sure I'll love it," I reply, as I tear the wrapping paper from the package. Inside, I find a tiny blue-and-white tea set. As I examine each piece, I notice that the design is not perfectly applied and that the edges of the cups are not smooth. "Wow," I say. "Thanks, Susan. I love it." I give my sister a hug, but on the inside, I wonder why she has given me a present that is so poorly made. I place the tea set in the family room corner cupboard and think to myself, "Susan was right. I am disappointed."

It is now some three months later, March 29, 1991. It is a cold, dreary day, and it has been raining for weeks. "Bye, sweetie. Have fun!" Susan says to me as I walk out the door. I am on my way to an Easter party at a friend's house, and Susan is planning to go out for the day, as well. As I leave through the back porch, I turn around to see Susan at the kitchen window. She is singing and swaying to the local country radio station as she washes the breakfast dishes for my mother. I catch her eye, and she flashes me one last smile.

While I spent the day playing Easter games without a care in the world, Susan's sixteen-year-old life was violently taken away from her. While driving with a friend along a wet road, Susan's car hydroplaned, spun out of control and fell off a forty-foot cliff to land in a river below. Susan's friend was thrown from the car, and he died instantly. Susan was not so lucky. Instead, she suffered severe head injuries, and after remaining in a complete coma for several months, she finally opened her eyes. Despite our hopes for a miraculous recovery, Susan spent the rest of her life in a vegetative state. Susan, my beloved Susan, could not function at all. Although we traveled to rehabilitation centers all over the East Coast with her, she never improved.

Two years after the initial accident, Susan died. She died at home in her bed, surrounded by the people who loved her. I held my sister's hand and looked into her eyes as she died. Susan's eyes seemed to talk to me, and I wanted nothing more than to make her wake up so that I could hear her comforting voice one last time. If I just looked into her eyes, I could still see the same Susan who always had a smile for everyone she met. Although her brain had been destroyed, and her body lingered on the verge of death, her eyes still talked to me. They reassured me and evoked feelings in me that are simply indescribable.

Several weeks after Susan died, I came across the miniature tea set in the family room corner cupboard. I had nearly forgotten about its existence, but seeing it again brought back instant memories. I held the flawed tea set in my hands and could once again feel the sweetness of my sister who loved everyone and everything. Perhaps she saw charm in the tea set's imperfect pieces, or perhaps she felt sorry for it, but either way, its flaws had not mattered to her.

Again, I am sitting at the desk in my room. Calmed by memories, I am no longer panicking over my literary analysis paper. Instead, I am holding the tea set and remembering Susan. I think I have finally received the true present that Susan gave me with the tea set over seven years ago, for I can now see beauty in nearly everyone I meet and appreciate things that most people dismiss as worthless. Just as its slanted, faded pattern and worn edges make my tea set beautiful, I now realize that true beauty lies in the imperfections and idiosyncrasies that make everyone special and unique.

The ability to see beauty in all people and things is not the only lesson that Susan taught me. She also made me realize that life is far too short and unpredictable to waste time worrying about insignificant things, and that true happiness lies in taking joy in life's simple pleasures. Susan lived her life this way, rarely letting arduous responsibilities detract from her ebullience, joy and compassion. With Susan smiling down on me, I finish my paper, turn off the computer and get into bed. Images of the beautiful tea set linger in my mind, and memories of Susan and my family soon flood my body with warmth. I realize all the beauty I have seen in my life; I smile and I am happy.

Laura Glenn Thornhill

Cotton Candy

When you're young you're told to be more responsible and act mature. If I knew being mature
meant realizing all the hardships both in the
world and in my life, I would have stayed three
years old.

Claudia Cicciarella

Dear Chicken Soup for the Teenage Soul,

I was only eight years old when I was forced to
grow up. My childhood dreams quickly became
adolescent responsibilities. In September of 1991 I
realized that the world is full of suffering, and it
took me seven years to realize that it is also full of
overcoming it.

My parents had separated that year. My sisters and I spent the first few months after the separation with my mom at her friend's house. Eventually we settled into a condominium of our own. We lived with my mom during the week and my dad on the weekends. Fridays were so hard. It was always so difficult to say good-bye to my mom. I could see the pain and anger in her eyes each time we would leave. My heart would ache tremendously. It always seemed like she looked at me as if it was the last time she would ever lay eyes on me. That made me even sadder.

One weekend, I decided not to say good-bye; I guess I was just trying to spare myself the pain. I got in the car with my father and we left, but as we were pulling away, I caught her sorrowful eyes as she watched us drive out of her life.

That weekend, my dad took us to a carnival at our synagogue. He seemed to be acting kind of strange, but we just tried to enjoy ourselves anyway. My dad was strict when it came to eating sugar, but on this day he let us eat cotton candy. I remember being flawlessly happy at that moment and my sisters' faces smiling at me with big bites of pink cotton in their mouths and joy in their eyes. Unfortunately, the happiness ended when we got home. My father sat us all down in the family room. As he spoke, his voice quivered in an obvious attempt to contain some unimaginable pain. He told us to always remember how happy we were that day and to never lose that. He then told us that our mother had committed suicide that morning.

The unbearable and intense pain I felt that day stayed with me for several years, and as the sorrow turned to anger, I learned to hate. I was furious with the idea that my mother had abandoned us. We were left to go through the turmoil of adolescence alone and unguided, to raise ourselves. From this loss, I learned not to trust anyone, for no one stays around forever. I constantly tested my friends' loyalty by pushing them away to see if they would come back. In the end, I always ended up alone. I hated everyone for leaving me—my friends, my mother, and even God. I was too bitter and too empty to realize that life can go on, but somewhere in the hollowness of my heart I finally found the strength to move forward. Heart Warrior Chosa once said, "In the darkest hour the soul is replenished and given strength to continue and endure."

I was touched by Jack Cavanaugh's story, "I'll Be Back,"* in *Chicken Soup for the Teenage Soul* about a boy who had lost his leg in a car accident. The boy, who was once the starting center on his

---

"I'll Be Back," by Jack Cavanaugh, Chicken Soup for the Teenage Soul, *pp. 279–286.*

high-school varsity basketball team, was hospitalized, had three operations, and ended up getting a prosthetic leg. He kept his spirits up and shunned anyone who told him that he would never play again. With determination, he did play basketball again. He wasn't bitter or angry, and he never pitied himself. He thanked God for saving his life, rather than hating God for taking his leg.

That's when I realized that I have everything it takes to overcome my anger and loneliness. God gives every soul the strength to endure; what was blinding me was my negative frame of mind. I now believe that anyone who experiences the kind of pain I did is also given the potential to overcome it. Seven years ago my mother died, and it is only recently that I have been able to overcome my anger, and trust my family, my friends and God once again. One day I hope to again feel as happy as I was with my first taste of cotton candy.

Thanks so much,
Michelle Sander

There for My Father

Dear Chicken Soup for the Teenage Soul,

I am a seventeen-year-old senior at the Accelerated Learning Center in Phoenix, Arizona. I just received *Chicken Soup for the Teenage Soul III,* and I am so thankful that these books exist. I had previously read the first two, and each one has helped me so much.

My father has been very ill for over three years now, and his illness has taken its toll on my family's emotional well-being. His troubles began when he had his first heart attack and was hospitalized for nearly a month. My emotions were running wild at that time, but I managed to get my hands on the first *Chicken Soup for the Teenage Soul.* It feels like I read it over a thousand times because it was my resource for coping with all the stress and pressure I felt dealing with my father's illness.

After my dad returned home from the hospital his health didn't really improve; instead, he seemed to get sicker. He could no longer do the things he was used to doing. Doctors ran additional tests on him and began kidney dialysis, which made him extremely weak and tired. It was around this time that I had saved up enough money to buy the *Chicken Soup for the Teenage Soul Journal*. I was feeling a bit rebellious then, which is evident by what I wrote in the *Journal*. I moved out of the house thinking that would reduce the stress on my mom and dad. The effect was quite the opposite. I realized they needed me more than any other time in their lives so I returned home after a short period away. It was hard, but I knew what had to be done. I was just having such a difficult time seeing my father go through so much agony that it broke my heart.

As time went on he continued to encounter more complications and even fell, hitting his head. He was okay, but my mother and I worried even more, which made my father become more upset than he already was. He wasn't angry at us for being so worried, instead he was frustrated that he was creating so much tension in our lives and he was so sorry for that.

Just recently he had another heart attack. He was released from the hospital shortly after that. It sort of felt like the doctors were throwing in the towel and saying there wasn't anything more they could do. He was in and out of the hospital a few more times for tests.

One day when I was on my way home from the market I turned the corner on my street and saw an ambulance and a fire truck outside of my house. It was like all the anger and frustration I had pent up inside of me exploded and I went ballistic. I could no longer hold it in anymore. A part of me blames myself for my father's condition because there is nothing I can do to help him to regain his health. Doctors have said that he cannot work or do anything that may be hard on him. They aren't even sure how much longer he will live. So, we are now forced to sell our house because my mother's income is not enough to support the family. When my father comes home from the hospital I feel guilty because I am not always happy to see him return. It's not that I don't want to see him—I do. It's just seeing him suffer so much that tears me up inside. I try to keep myself occupied as much as possible away from my home so I don't have to see him in pain and my mother in tears. My father holds a tremendous amount of guilt because he feels like his condition is always upsetting my mother. He seems to lose his temper more than he ever did, and that is understandable. But he yells at me now, which he never used to do. I have always been daddy's little girl. However, we all continue to get through this and keep as much of a positive attitude as we can.

Having just gotten *Chicken Soup for the Teenage Soul III,* I feel a little bit of relief. It has helped me keep my mind off of certain things and to reduce my stress level. Just knowing that other teenagers my age are going through or have gone through a similar situation and have come out of it okay is encouraging.

I admire what you guys are doing for teenagers. You have realized that we, too, need support systems. I have learned not to blame myself for what is happening, but to try and find the good in these types of situations. I am learning to cherish the happy moments I have. I know that being stubborn is not going to do me any good. I try to talk to my father more and let him know that I love him, even if I have to say it twenty times each minute. It is important that he knows.

I hope you are already working on the fourth book, because I will be the first one in line to get it.

Sincerely,
Samantha Yeomans

Coping with the Loss of a Friend

Dear Chicken Soup for the Teenage Soul,

So often it takes a tragic event to cause someone to look more closely at his or her life. My life seemed to be cruising along in happy mode when suddenly my world was rocked by the death of one of my best friends.

Her name was Heather Marshall, and she battled cystic fibrosis for most of her life. Even though I knew she had the disease, I guess I was just hopeful there would never be a day when I would have to go to her funeral.

I had just returned home from a laughter-filled night out with some other friends when I received the worst news of my life. There was a message on my answering machine that at first sounded like laughter, but as I listened more carefully I realized it was my other friend, Heather Correll, sobbing with tremendous agony. She said that Heather was dead. I immediately stopped in my tracks thinking it was all just a bad dream. I had to rewind the tape five times to convince myself that what I was hearing was true. The room seemed like it was spinning, and tears blurred my vision. I didn't know how to react except to cry. I dropped to my knees in a clump, hitting the floor. At that point my mom walked in and she immediately asked me what was wrong. I told her, and she looked at me stunned, but at the same time very concerned, knowing how much pain I was in. After things began to sink in, I called all my friends who were close to Heather so we could share our sorrow together.

A memorial for Heather was held later that week. I made a promise to myself and to Heather that I would not go to her memorial crying and full of sadness, since she had told me before her death that when she died she would be in a better place. When I got to the memorial there was an overwhelming feeling of sadness in the room. Even though all these people were gathered to mourn her death, the full impact of her not being here anymore hadn't hit me yet—until I was in line to sign the book for Heather's family. As I approached the table, there were several pictures of Heather when she was younger. I could no longer hold it in, and I began to cry. As I made my way to a seat, some friends joined me. We exchanged hellos and hugged each other as a group. The room once again felt like it was spinning, much like my room had felt when I first received the news of her death. My mind flashed back to the good times Heather and I had growing up, when we would get in trouble for laughing in class because she stuck a pencil up her nose, or when Lindsey had made a funny comment about a teacher. It seemed then like we would be friends forever and nothing could tear us apart.

Several people spoke at her memorial. We were told that Heather had kept a journal with a "good day" section and a "bad day" section. What amazed me was even though she endured years of treatments, IV machines and hospital visits, she never once wrote in the "bad day" section. To know that she lived such a happy life, despite that horrible disease, brought me some much-needed comfort.

It has been nearly two-and-a-half years since Heather passed away, and I still think about her often. I have learned so much from her. She knew that she would probably die at an early age, but she still managed to always keep a positive attitude. She made her short life here the best it could possibly be, and that to me is very admirable. She has taught me not to take things for granted, and that I need to make the most of my life and enjoy it to the fullest. I tell myself and others that no matter who you are—even if you have a life-threatening disease or are "different from other kids"—you are still someone. Life may not always seem so great and things may not always go your way, but just remember you were brought into this world for a reason.

Just like Heather has taught me to be strong, the *Chicken Soup for the Teenage Soul* books have given me strength to deal with her death, to look at it from a more positive perspective and to be optimistic. When someone dies, it can hurt a lot and be confusing, but dwelling on those negative feelings isn't healthy. There are so many great memories I have of Heather, and I choose to think about those instead and know that she is still with us.

Thanks so much,
Courtney Day

Letting Go of Guilt

Dear Teenage Chicken Soup,

I haven't finished reading the entire book, *Chicken Soup for the Teenage Soul,* but it has inspired me already. I went straight to the Tough Stuff chapter. I am seventeen years old and have experienced many tough times.

Just recently, I was involved in a fatal car accident in which two people were killed. I was the one driving, but I still don't know how it happened. The passengers in our car were my two cousins, my cousin's boyfriend, and his brother and girlfriend. My cousin's boyfriend's brother and girlfriend were the two passengers who died. It was weird because no one blamed me except myself. I did not know how I was going to deal with it. I had help from my family and friends, but I knew that I was the only one who could help myself. I didn't think anyone understood what I was actually going through. For a while, I thought I was doing fine, but I would have emotional breakdowns in the middle of the night. No one even knew this. I felt guilty that I had survived and two people did not. I couldn't help but wonder why them and not me, and I couldn't stop blaming myself. I am only seventeen, and I have seen and experienced something so incredibly tragic and horrible.

I bought your book because I was reading pieces of it in a bookstore. While reading "Dead at 17,"* I thought of my accident. It made me cry hard, for a long time. I hadn't cried like that since the accident, and it felt better to just let it out.

I have now realized that maybe there was a reason I didn't die in the accident. The "On Learning" chapter has also taught me that I must learn from this. I can't just sulk around and not do anything for my future. I just want to thank you and everyone who put their efforts into this inspirational book. It has really given me hope. It's good to know that some people really do care about what some teenagers are going through. This book has put a smile on my face and allowed me to feel happy that I'm alive.

Love,
Myrna Yuson

---

*"Dead at 17," by John Berrio, Chicken Soup for the Teenage Soul, pp. 226–227.

The Crash

Dear Chicken Soup,

Today I bought *Chicken Soup for the Teenage Soul II*. I am already on page twenty, and I can't put the book down!

I recently watched a boy a few years older than me die on the side of the road because he and his friends had been drinking and took a turn at ninety miles per hour and crashed into another car. I was the first one at the scene and called 911. My boyfriend and I were going home after Homecoming, an unforgettable night. We were just talking and laughing when we both saw the crash. I heard screeching and screaming. We drove up to where the cars had hit, and I got out of the car. While I was dialing 911, I looked down and realized I was standing barefoot in glass and gasoline.

My boyfriend went to the cars to see if everyone was all right. In the car that got hit by the teenagers were three older ladies. They were all okay at the time. But, unfortunately, one of the ladies died about a week after the accident.

The boys in the other car were both unconscious. I stood there watching paramedics try to keep the driver of the car alive. Ten minutes later they put a body bag over him. I will never forget the boy who died or the blood and glass everywhere and the bottle of alcohol the police took out of the car.

To this day I will never let any of my friends drive drunk or drive with someone who has been drinking. I do not want to lose someone I love. Watching that boy die made me realize how easily life can be taken away. This really proved to me how stupid drinking is.

I just wanted to tell you my experience and how reading your book really helped me think about the whole situation. I hope I can share it with others.

Sincerely,
Elizabeth Young

When I Get Out

To the Authors of
Chicken Soup for the Teenage Soul,

I am a fifteen-year-old girl serving time in a juvenile detention facility in Washington. I have seen a
lot for my young age. I started doing drugs heavily
in seventh grade. In eighth grade, I started throwing up my food, starving myself, popping diet pills
and speed, snorting lines of crank and crystal
meth, and cutting myself. I was five feet, seven
inches tall and eighty-five pounds when I was
admitted to the psychiatric unit of the hospital.

I didn't really learn anything even after I was dis-
charged because I ran with gangs and continued
taking drugs. Life was a party. The gangs I knew
were my family. I was both physically and verbally
abusive to my mom, who loved me the most. One

night I needed a place to stay so some guys picked up me and my friends, and we broke into a house and had a big party. We found a gun while everyone was getting drunk, and we played with it. The cops came the next day and, though we had thought of stealing the gun, we didn't—but someone else did.

Now I am stuck here, charged with first-degree burglary of a firearm, even though I never took the gun. I will have the record forever. I face the chance of being sent to adult prison for five years. I do take full responsibility for the events that led up to the gun being stolen. I know that no one could have saved me, but myself—and I failed.

While I do my time, I read, and my mom bought me your book, *Chicken Soup for the Teenage Soul*. It's such a good book to have in this place, and something I really needed. I especially liked the story "Unconditional Mom."* I have laughed *and* cried while reading this book. It has made me rethink what I want my life to be when I get out. I do know I want to change. I'm a smart person who made stupid choices and lots of mistakes. I am grateful I'll be given a second chance.

Thanks for this book and thanks for listening.

Sincerely,
Lisa McKinney

---

* *"Unconditional Mom," by Sarah J. Vogt,* Chicken Soup for the Teenage Soul, *pp. 74–77.*

$\overline{6}$

HELPING
OTHERS

When we do for others, we can't help but be
   touched by the love and generosity we thought
   we were giving away.

Kimberly Kirberger

Helping Others: Introduction

One of the things that gives us great pleasure as *Chicken Soup for the Soul* authors is that we donate a large portion of the proceeds from each book to charity. With the teenage series we choose organizations that work directly with teenagers. We searched long and hard to find people who really cared about teens and who also greatly needed the money. In each case, we wanted to know that our donation would make a difference. We couldn't be happier with the results. It is a great feeling to be able to support people who are dedicated to teens and working so hard on their behalf.

We have chosen to give the charity money from this book to two organizations we have worked with in the past, as well as some new organizations and individuals, all of whom we are thrilled to be able to support.

The following chapter is about these amazing people and the work they do. We know you will be inspired by their stories and will join us in supporting them in any way you can.

If you would like to make a small donation, start a group at your school or write a letter of thanks to the following people, their contact information is included following their letters.

Mike's Gift: A Continuation of the Story "Hero of the 'Hood"*

Dear Chicken Soup for the Teenage Soul Readers,

The first time I met Mike Powell, I had driven north at dawn from Mexico where I live to interview this unknown teenager in South Central Los Angeles. I'd heard from a friend of a friend that Mike had an interesting life story, and finding interesting stories is how I make my living. I've been good at it and, in twenty-five years of being a writer, I've been told that my stories have changed some people's lives. Only this story, though, changed my *own* life forever.

Late on the night of the interview, as I drove back home in the dark, I couldn't concentrate on the

* *"Hero of the 'Hood," by Paula McDonald,* Chicken Soup for the Teenage Soul II, *pp. 148–155.*

music playing in my car. My mind was reeling from what I'd heard that day, and the information flying around in my head wouldn't drop into the familiar cubbyholes we all use to categorize things. It was too bizarre. Too awful.

At first, interviewing this big, shy seventeen-year-old had been like pulling teeth. Then, little by little, as he opened up and started to trust me, bits and pieces of his story started tumbling out at random. I was stunned, mesmerized and sickened, all at the same time. For a long time, I'd had this image of myself as so worldly, so cool. I thought I'd been just about everywhere, heard just about everything and that not much could still throw me. But, from this gentle, soft-spoken young man, I learned that day—and on so many subsequent days in the years to follow—that there was another whole world out there I'd never even dreamed existed. A world worse than anything I'd ever seen on television; worse than anything I'd ever read about war. And it was peopled by children like Mike and his siblings who thought the world they lived in was normal.

That was five years ago, and I've since come to think of the young man who sat across a kitchen table and talked with me that day as a miracle of some sort. Not just because he had survived the ugliness that engulfed him and was still alive to tell about it, but because he wasn't bitter or angry. Instead, he was filled with a sweetness and love and acceptance of life I'd never experienced in someone who had been kicked around so badly. Here was a person who had lost his entire childhood, but, "hey, it was gone," he'd shrug and smile. "I need to get past that and get on," he'd say. For me, and evidently for so many of you who wrote to me after reading Mike's story, learning about those first seventeen years was an emotionally wrenching, eye-opening view of a totally alien world. Mike might as well have existed on another planet, populated by real monsters and the stuff of nightmares. For those of you who haven't had a chance to read *Chicken Soup for the Teenage Soul II* yet, "Hero of the 'Hood" will be shocking.

Trapped in Los Angeles' worst slum, this young boy made a conscious decision at the age of nine that cost him his childhood and so much more. He was just a little kid, but he stepped forward at that moment in time to take sole responsibility for his family of seven younger siblings. He then proceeded to successfully raise them—alone—in a world of crime, danger and poverty. Brutalized by a drug-dealing father and later by a terrifying, cocaine-pushing stepfather, he survived the treachery and abandonment of a crack-addicted mother and the daily gangland violence and slayings that surrounded them all. For an incredible eight years, the authorities (schools, teachers, social workers, the police) never learned that one young street kid was the only parent this family had and that he was their sole emotional and financial support. Beware. This is no fairy tale. It is a chronicle of murder, suicide, rage, constant fear, true evil and remarkable courage. Mike Powell was shot eight times before he was fifteen—just trying to keep his family alive and together. His story is a startlingly different picture of America in the 1990s than the one most of us know.

Here's just one short excerpt from the original story that gives a glimpse into what it's like to have crack addicts as parents and to be terrorized continually by a junkie, out of control. And remember, we're talking about a nine-year-old here who has to keep his entire life a secret because he's trying desperately to keep his family from being broken up and having his little brother and six sisters put in separate foster homes.

To make sure no one suspected anything, Mike began cleaning the apartment himself, doing laundry by hand and keeping his sisters fed, diapered and immaculate. He scavenged junk shops for hairbrushes, bottles and clothes, whatever they could afford, and covered up for his mother's absences with an endless litany of excuses. Cheryl and Marcel were soon burning through everything the family had in order to buy crack—even money for rent and the children's food. When their money situation became desperate, Mike quietly quit elementary school at nine to support the family himself. He cleaned yards, unloaded trucks and stocked liquor stores, always working before dawn or late at night so the smaller children wouldn't be alone while awake.

As Cheryl and Marcel's drug binges and absences became longer and more frequent, their brief returns became more violent. Sinking deeper into addiction, Cheryl would simply abandon Marcel when his drugs ran out and hook up with someone who was better supplied. A crazed Marcel would then rampage through the slum apartment, torturing and terrorizing the children for information about where more money was hidden or where he could find their mother.

One night, Marcel put Mike's two-year-old sister in a plastic bag and held it closed. Without air, the toddler's eyes were bulging and she was turning blue. "Where's your mother?" the addict screamed.

Sobbing, Mike and little five-year-old Raf threw themselves at Marcel again and again, beating on his back with small, ineffectual fists. In desperation, Mike finally sank his teeth into Marcel's neck, praying the savage tormenter would drop the plastic bag and pick on him instead. It worked. Marcel wheeled and threw Mike through the window, cutting him with shattered glass and breaking his arm.

The story gets worse. A lot worse, as many of you already know.

More than a thousand of you from all over the world wrote to me after reading "Hero of the 'Hood": ordinary suburban kids from cities and small towns all over America who were as shocked as I was by the brutality of the story. Teachers, parents and church groups wrote, as well as teens from India, Malaysia, the United Kingdom, Australia and everywhere else the *Chicken Soup* books traveled. Your questions were often the same: "Is Mike real or was that just fiction?" "What's happened to them all now?" "How can I write to Mike to tell him how incredible I think he is?" And, in different words, in different dialects, in scribbled, penciled notes or beautifully typed letters on corporate stationery, in hundreds and hundreds and hundreds of e-mails, there was almost always the same basic message for me to pass on: "Please tell Mike that he's inspired me more than anyone I've ever read about. I thought I had it bad. Wow! Was I wrong. I'll never take my life for granted again. Please tell him that."

I did. Every letter, every postcard, every e-mail I got was printed out or copied and put in my "Mike" pile. Once a month, I'd send those amazing letters north so that he'd know that his struggle had had meaning for others. And whenever I drove up to see him, I'd take the latest pile along and read them out loud to him and his family so they'd all know.

Mike's story made many of you cry. Many of *your* letters made me cry. By the time I started receiving them, I'd known Mike for almost three years. But, suddenly, I was now getting to know you, too, and seeing Mike again, but through your eyes.

Emily wrote:

My name is Emily Spence, and I am thirteen years old and I live in Memphis, Tennessee. I just wanted to tell you that I thought your story "Hero of the 'Hood" was so moving. I don't know that I've ever heard a story that inspirational before. Although I really don't know much about that kind of life, I realize how good I have it and how much I have been sheltered—not by any ONE person, but by society. Anyway, just wanted to tell you that I truly appreciate your writing that story. It really meant something to me. Thanks, Emily

In the last three years, I've answered every letter and e-mail. When you write, I fill you in on what's transpired in Mike's life since the story was published, because so many of you have asked what's happening now to Mike and his whole family. Well, they're getting there, little by little, but life doesn't always provide happy endings right away. Unfortunately, the real world isn't like a sitcom that ends neat and clean each week.

Mike's grandmother, Mabel, is almost seventy now, and she still has to work full-time, which means commuting more than one hundred miles a day, then coming home to take care of the kids in the evening. She sleeps about four hours a night. Mike's grandfather, Otis, who has been taking care of the youngest kids during the day for the last few years while Mabel and Mike work, was recently diagnosed with cancer. Otis has already had surgery several times and now lives in constant pain. I don't think he sleeps much at all these days. The kids are safe, though, at last, and happy in a whole new world without constant violence surrounding them. They're out of the 'hood, out of daily danger, and finally out of the clutches of Marcel and their mother. All of them are doing great in school, and not one of those eight kids (three of whom are now teenagers) has ever been in any kind of trouble. That's an incredible credit to Mike and the values he instilled in them.

Mike's own life hasn't been easy these past few years, either, even with his grandparents now helping with the kids. (In case you've never thought about this, when you drop out of school at nine, finding decent work as an adult is incredibly difficult.) Mike's had to work his way through a series of minimum-wage jobs and has frequently worked two and three different jobs a day to make enough money to help keep the family going. Right now, he works a twelve-hour shift, sometimes more, and still has to make time to study and get special tutoring for all the years of school he missed. But, Mike is determined to catch up. He just passed the preliminary tests for his GED, and soon the phone is going to ring down here, and he's going to tell me that he finally got that high school equivalency. Believe me, when that happens, we're all going to have one big celebration.

When some of you received updates from me about Mike, you were troubled by the fact that the story didn't have a completely happy ending yet.

That's good. I'm glad so many of you are thinking about how long it sometimes takes to fix the really hard things in life. And that it takes an unbelievable amount of work and perseverance and drive to go back and try to get something later in life that most of us take for granted early on. Like an education. And that it can take years, or even a lifetime, to make up for a lost youth.

Most people don't realize that everything about writing changes the writer in some ways, too, and that includes your letters to me. Sometimes, when I write back to readers to update them on Mike, their second responses are even more beautiful and moving than their original letters, like this one from Jaclyn:

Dear Paula,

Thank you so much for your reply. I'm glad that Mike's life is now in order, although he must be pretty tired out when he gets home from work! I feel really bad for his grandpa. Three years ago, when I was in grade five, I had a brain tumor that was cancerous. It was a very scary time for my family as well as me. I know what Mike and his family are going through and I want them to know that they are not alone. I will pray for Mike and his family as it sounds like they could use a lot of prayer right now. I will probably mail Mike a little letter to let him know that lots of people know about his story and are praying for him. My name is Jaclyn Taekema and I live in British Columbia. If you see Mike anytime soon, could you please tell him that he is being prayed for in Canada? Thank you so much again for your reply.

There is one extra-special letter that I've kept pinned up on the wall over my desk since I got it. It was sent to me by an organization that asked me to pass their letter on to Mike because he didn't have an address at that time. The first two paragraphs contain some of the most beautiful words I've ever read.

Dear Michael,

It is my pleasure to inform you that you have been selected to receive one of the 1998 America's Awards. Known as 'The Nobel Prize for Goodness,' this award is presented each year to six unsung heroes who personify the American character and spirit. Recipients are 'ordinary' people who are extraordinary examples of this nation's values. You were chosen from 688 candidates by our Story Judges and by our Blue-Ribbon Selection Committee.

The letter was signed by Elizabeth Peale Allen, chairperson of the Positive Thinking Foundation and the daughter of Norman Vincent Peale.

Mike received his America's Award in Palm Springs, California, on January 30, 1999. My husband and I were there that night to applaud and cheer and jump up and down because something truly wonderful was finally happening to the most deserving person I've ever known. Driving back from Palm Springs that night, I had a chance to think about how I've changed in the time Mike and I have known each other and about the gift of perspective he's given me. It's been five years since that first interview across a kitchen table. I've spent a lot of time with Mike and his family around other kitchen tables since then, and we've become close friends. Right now, I'm writing a book about Mike's life because I've learned so much more than I knew when I first wrote that short article about him for *Chicken Soup*. The rest of the story is so devastating, so unimaginably awful, and yet so ultimately triumphant and beautiful, that it continues to astonish me—and to break my heart. But, even in the retelling of the worst of these most deeply buried horrors, Mike's never complained about what a tough hand he was dealt in life. I don't think he ever will. And that's what still gets to me every time.

When I make those long drives home from Los Angeles today, I still turn off the CD player, just as I did the first time, and I drive through the night thinking about Mike's life and my own. About how lucky I've been every step of the way. And about how often I've taken the ordinary things for granted, like reading a book, or simply opening a refrigerator, or having a bed and shoes, and even being able to get out of the rain. And I vow, once again, not to complain about the stupid, petty, inconsequential and often fleeting things that sometimes get me down. Or to take my own very good life for granted.

And whenever I think I'm having a bad day, I try to remember that I don't even have a clue what a really bad day is. Nobody's ever thrown me through a window. Nobody's ever stomped deliberately on my already broken ankle just to hurt me more. Nobody's ever put me in a garbage Dumpster at midnight and made me dig for food for my family.

No, I honestly really don't know what a bad day is. And the one person I know in this world who actually does know never spends any time whining about it or blaming others. So, I think about these things driving through the dark, and I think about your letters. And I vow each time the sun comes up that I'm going to try to be a better person. I'm going to try to be more like Mike.

Sincerely,
Paula McDonald

Helping Others

Chicken Soup for the Soul will donate a portion of the proceeds from this book to Mike and his family. Once we encounter true goodness, it is like a virus. One is susceptible to catching it no matter what the circumstances.

There Is Hope

Dear Kimberly,

I am writing in response to *Chicken Soup for the Teenage Soul*. I am a teacher for the Delaware County Juvenile Detention Center located in Muncie, Indiana. I work with juveniles who are currently awaiting detention hearings. These juveniles have various charges such as runaway, theft, battery, possession of marijuana/cocaine and criminal mischief. They often come from homes of violence and neglect. The majority of the juveniles have either been suspended or expelled from their schools, or have quit school altogether. They have little self-esteem or self-discipline and do not have academic goals. When asked about life plans or longevity, they show no hope or enthusiasm for their futures.

As an educator, I often feel helpless and discouraged with this student population. The students come from such diverse backgrounds that I need materials that bridge their differences and provide a common ground for discussion and icebreakers. *Chicken Soup for the Teenage Soul* has come to my rescue many times. This book is one of the few tools I can use in the detention classroom that will actually spark interest or a glimpse of emotion. Even those students who have not previously shown any effort to read or to check out library books will specifically ask for your teenage helping. It is amazing to see a juvenile laughing to himself in his seat or to see tears welling up in the eyes of a student who has tried so hard for so long to hide her feelings.

I will never forget one very depressed and distraught student. She refused to participate in class, counseling or recreation. She had come to us with a list of charges and was awaiting a court date. She appeared tired all the time and had obviously given up on all adults. Finally, she was introduced to your book in our classroom. She began copying poems, reading the stories and, finally, sharing her favorites with the other students. Because of the book's ability to expose her loneliness she found a common ground that allowed her to discuss and share her feelings with others.

Thank you. Thank you for proving to me that no matter where a juvenile has come from, what they have experienced, or where they are going, they can still be reached. They have hearts yearning to be touched. I will continue to use your books in the detention center classroom, encouraging each student to read a selection. I am very appreciative of your stories, and I know my students gratefully thank you as well.

Sincerely,
Kari J. Lee

Helping Others

We have received hundreds of letters from teachers similar to this one. We are currently working on a project called "Soup and Support for Teachers," which will give teachers the opportunity to use these books free of charge along with a guidebook called *101 Ways to Use Chicken Soup in the Classroom*. If you would like to know more about this program and find out ways you can help or to be a recipient of this program, contact:

Soup and Support for Teachers
P.O. Box 999
Pacific Palisades, CA 90272
310-573-3655

Also, we have sent a classroom set of books to Delaware County Juvenile Detention Center in Kari Lee's name, and she will be a contributor to our *101 Ways* guidebook.

Yellow Ribbon Project

Dear Kim, Jack and Mark,

We received an e-mail today from a boy who had just finished reading our story in *Chicken Soup for the Teenage Soul*. He had planned on committing suicide last night, but he had flipped through the "Tough Stuff" section in the book—and realized that hurting himself wasn't the answer. He asked us to send him some yellow ribbon cards and thanked us for saving his life.

Although astonishing in itself, this is just one example of the thousands of letters, calls and e-mails we have received since the inclusion of our story in the *Chicken Soup for the Teenage Soul* book. Thousands of lives have been saved as a result of our inspired partnership, and it is in the spirit of profound gratitude that we write to you today.

As you know, in September of 1994 we experienced the greatest loss a parent can face—the death of a child. In the depths of despair our beloved son, Mike, shot himself in the front seat of his cherished yellow Mustang. He took his life when he did not know the words to say, or how to let someone know he was in trouble and needed help. Stories of Mike's life and humble generosity poured in from friends and mourners. In the midst of our suffering, we were nurtured by the awareness that at such a young age Mike had truly made a difference in so many people's lives. Our grief seemed insurmountable and our loss unbearable. Yet somehow, in our darkest hours, we held on to a tiny ray of light, the hope that we could somehow continue Mike's legacy of giving and making a difference. We thought up the idea for a card that would allow teens to ask for help when they are unable to express themselves with words. Thus, the Yellow Ribbon Project was born from our intense desire for no teen to have to go through what Mike had—and no parent to have to experience the pain we were feeling. The Yellow Ribbon Project has been our solace and our mission.

When our story was told in *A 3rd Serving of Chicken Soup for the Soul*, the letters and calls poured in. We were humbled and energized by the response, and we worked even harder to get the cards out to people and spread the message. We realized how many children and teens were suffering all over the country, and our desire to help grew. When Kim called to ask us to tell the story in our own words for *Chicken Soup for the Teenage Soul*,* we were stunned and thrilled. In some ways, we were still just two grieving parents who missed their son, so when we received that call from Kim and knew that we were being given the opportunity to reach and potentially help millions of teens, we were awestruck. After hours of conversation with Kim, we formed a friendship and connection that has lasted to this day. We will never forget the day she called to tell us that our organization had been chosen as the recipient of a portion of proceeds from the book. To say we were astounded by the news would be an understatement. When she came up to Colorado to present us with the first check, we knew Mike's legacy of making a difference would be felt around the globe.

They say it takes a village to raise a child. We add that it takes a village to save a child. Our partnership with *Chicken Soup for the Teenage Soul* has done wonders for children and teens all over the global village. Together we have saved lives. We

---

* *"I'll Always Be with You,"* by Dale and Dar Emme, Chicken Soup for the Teenage Soul, *pp. 206–210.*

505526 6582

READER/CUSTOMER CARE SURVEY

We care about your opinions. Please take a moment to fill out this Reader Survey card and mail it back to us.
As a special **"thank you"** we'll send you exciting news about interesting books and a valuable **Gift Certificate**

Please PRINT using ALL CAPITALS

Name

First   MI.⌷   Last
                                                 Name

Address

City   ST ⌷   Zip

Phone # (⌷⌷⌷) ⌷⌷⌷ - ⌷⌷⌷⌷   Fax # (⌷⌷⌷) ⌷⌷⌷ - ⌷⌷⌷⌷

Email

(1) Gender: **(2) Age:**
O Girl   O 9-12   O 31+
O Boy   O 13-16
               O 17-20
               O 21-30

(3) Who purchased this book?
O You   O Relative
O Parent   O Adult Friend
O Grandparent O Counselor or Teacher
O Friend

(4) Was this book bought as a gift?
O Yes   O No

(5) How did you find out about this book?
Please fill in ONE.
O Friend   O Radio
O School   O Counselor
O Parent   O Teen Magazine Ad

(6) What do you like to read?
Teen Magazines: Please fill in all that apply.
O Teen   O Teen Beat
O Seventeen   O All About You
O Teen People O Twist
O YM   O Christian Youth Magazines
O Jump   O Other:_____

Books: Please fill in all that apply.
O Fiction   O Sports
O Reality   O Non-Fiction

(20) Where do you usually buy books?
Please fill in your top TWO choices only.
O Bookstore
O Discount Store
O Grocery Store
O School Book Sale
O Websites
O Price Club

(22) How many books do you buy or read a month (not school books)?
O 1   O 3
O 2   O 4+

(23) Did you enjoy this book?
O Yes
O No
O Most

CA3

BUSINESS REPLY MAIL

FIRST-CLASS MAIL PERMIT NO 45 DEERFIELD BEACH, FL

POSTAGE WILL BE PAID BY ADDRESSEE

CHICKEN SOUP FOR THE TEENAGE LETTERS
HEALTH COMMUNICATIONS, INC.
3201 SW 15TH STREET
DEERFIELD BEACH FL 33442-9875

FOLD HERE

1708266583

(24) What are your TWO favorite TV Shows?

- ○ Dawson's Creek
- ○ Survivor
- ○ The Daly Show
- ○ The Simpsons
- ○ Friends
- ○ Buffy the Vampire Slayer
- ○ Will & Grace
- ○ Who wants to be a Millionaire
- ○ Other: _____

Do you have your own Chicken Soup story that you would like to send us?
Please submit separately to: Chicken Soup for the Soul, P.O. Box 30880,
Santa Barbara, CA 93130

**What do you think would be an interesting idea
for a book that is not currently available?**

CA3

keep a database of all the communication we have received. Of these, 1,247 people have written to tell us that they read the story in *Chicken Soup for the Teenage Soul* and decided not to end their lives. Imagine . . . 1,247 lives—that we know of—have been saved, all because we were given an opportunity to share our story with others.

There are nights we go to bed and think of all that's happened because of this tragedy—all the awareness that has been raised, the lives that have been saved, and the teens and parents who have been helped. It is an immense blessing to be able to help kids going through the same thing Mike was. To know that we are preventing other parents from going through the pain we have, to know that we are able to reach a child or teen at the perfect moment—these are the miracles that help our hearts to keep on loving. We are deeply indebted to *Chicken Soup* for the increased opportunities you have given us to channel the energy of our grief and suffering into that of giving and compassion. We thank you for your friendship and support.

With love and blessings,
Dale and Dar Emme

Helping Others

How does one even put into words the feelings that are generated by this letter? Their story, their generosity, their compassion and the miracles that have grown out of such an enormous tragedy continue to amaze us. From the moment we heard this story, we were overwhelmed by the Emmes' ability to deal with the loss of their son by deciding not only to help others, but to help others by talking about the circumstances of their son's death every single day. These are two amazing human beings and the work they are doing is truly making a difference. We have witnessed it ourselves. We have watched teenagers come up to them after a talk and just cry on their shoulders from the sorrow they feel about Mike. They feel safe with Dale and Dar because their sincerity is unmistakable.

We made the decision four years ago to help this small but inspired organization by donating a portion of the proceeds from the first *Chicken Soup for the Teenage Soul* book. We have always felt good about this decision and we have continued to donate proceeds from other *Chicken Soup for the Teenage Soul* books. It is with great joy that we chose them yet again to receive proceeds from this book. They are no longer the small organization that we originally chose to help, but they are definitely still the inspired one.

If you would like more information about the Yellow Ribbon Project, you may contact them at:

Yellow Ribbon Project
P.O. Box 644
Westminster, CO 80030
Phone: 303-429-3530
Fax: 303-426-4496
e-mail: *light4life@yellowribbon.org*
Web site: *www.yellowribbon.org*

We Did It!

Dear Chicken Soup for the Soul,

We started out so simple. As Daisies we were taught the basics of scouting. Selling cookies and learning manners were considered staples at age six. But we never expected, thirteen years later, that Girl Scouting would change us so much. Our turning point came, unexpectedly, by reading *Chicken Soup for the Teenage Soul*.

In the book, we read of a program known as the Yellow Ribbon Project—a teen suicide prevention program. The founders, Dar and Dale Emme, lost their teenage son, Mike, through teen suicide. We contacted the Emmes and decided that this program would be our donation to the community. We would create a teen suicide prevention program in Rockland County with the help of Dar and

Dale. As it turned out, the project was quite extensive and required an extraordinary amount of time and effort to be launched. Fortunately, our determination worked past these challenges. Teen suicide was at epidemic levels in our county. We agreed that it needed to be addressed.

Our primary concern was the amount of money three Girl Scouts, on their own, would be able to raise. We began by spending countless hours and weekends selling Girl Scout cookies to our community outside a local Grand Union. Eventually, when the cookies ran out, we found that people were just giving donations. As a community they had decided that we needed to stop this epidemic by supporting programs like ours.

Local businesses in our community readily agreed to help out. They donated above and beyond what was asked or expected. More than six thousand yellow ribbons were distributed to the community at large. Every single ribbon was made from materials that were donated. Hotels, airlines and fabric shops all helped generously so this dream could be realized.

The next step was coordinating schedules with our school systems. We needed to present the program so it would reach as many students as possible. The best method would be presentations at two local public schools and one local private high school. Despite the countless hours of fundraising and the donations of the community, we were still lacking substantial funds. Each school, after hours of discussion and debate, offered a monetary subsidy in return for the presentation.

After much anticipation and planning, our program was launched on October 5, 1999. In two days, we reached thirty-five hundred kids with the message that suicide is NOT an option. They were told that there is help available, there are people who care, and it is okay to ask for help. Each student left that day with a yellow ribbon card and the knowledge of how to use it.

We never asked the kids to thank us, but they did. From their expressions and responses, we received the greatest thanks of all. They listened, they learned and they stayed alive. We had gone from selling cookies to saving lives. With the help of Girl Scouts, *Chicken Soup for the Teenage Soul*, and Dar and Dale Emme, we'd reached our greatest achievement: We kept the message alive; suicide is not an option. And people *do* care.

Sincerely,
Natalie Cabrera, Deena Ecker and Amanda Nulman

[*Editors' Note:* If you want to start a Yellow Ribbon program in your community, please contact us or Dale and Dar Emme and we will do whatever we can to help.]

A Most Precious Possession

Dear Kimberly, Mark and Jack,

We lost one of the most precious possessions of our lives on August 4, 1999. Our seventeen-year-old daughter, Whitney, died suddenly and unexpectedly of an undetected heart condition, and our world seemed to disintegrate around us.

In the time since then, we have struggled to not only survive this awful experience, but also to look for blessings. We knew what an outstanding daughter we had and were searching for things that influenced her to be such a remarkable young lady. Many people have told us of thoughtful things she had done for others that we had no knowledge of. Since Whitney was always thinking of others, we established a scholarship fund in her name at Mount Vernon High School. We trust this will keep her memory alive while she continues to benefit others as she always did.

The purpose of our writing is to tell you the pleasure Whitney derived from reading your *Chicken Soup* books. She had read *Chicken Soup for the Teenage Soul* and *Chicken Soup for the Pet Lover's Soul* recently. In the book bag she had with her on her final day of life, she carried *Chicken Soup for the Teenage Soul II*. She was on her way to Cleveland with her gymnastics team to the Junior Olympic Gymnastic Meet when her death occurred. As was her pattern, only things dear to her ever made it into her gym bag. So we wanted you to know that her last days were spent with your wonderful books.

She had given me *Chicken Soup for the Mother's Soul* for Mother's Day in 1998 after I had been diagnosed with breast cancer. This book will always be special to me. Whitney was both a gifted athlete and an international baccalaureate honor student. We feel your writings helped make her what she was. Our hope is that you will continue the wonderful work you do for all and especially for teenagers.

Sincerely,
Sherry and Jerry Sharp

Helping Others

We were so touched to receive this letter and are honored to be able to make a gift of $1,000 to the memorial scholarship fund that has been established in Whitney's honor at International Gymnastics Camp. The fund provides tuition scholarships for children otherwise unable to afford gymnastics training at the camp. If you would like more information or would like to make a donation, please contact:

Whitney Sharp's Scholarship Fund
International Gymnastics Camp
9020 Bartonsville Woods Rd.
Stroudsburg, PA 18360

Challenge Day

Challenge Day is a miraculous workshop that transforms the lives of youth in a single day. Since its inception in 1987, the Challenge Day program has successfully demonstrated the power of possibility for hundreds of thousands of youth and adults across the nation. Through a series of games, activities and group discussion, Challenge Day breaks down the barriers that separate us as human beings. As a result, young people open their hearts and learn to trust, love and support each other in becoming the natural leaders that they are. Challenge Day successfully addresses the issues of violence, racism, teasing, stereotypes, tobacco, drugs and alcohol. Communities all over the country witness radical, positive changes in schools and families as a result of Challenge Days.

We chose a story about Challenge Day for one of our books. When we learned more about

Challenge Day and the profound impact it was having on teens all over the country, we chose them to receive a portion of the book's proceeds.

The following letter is from Yvonne St. John-Dutra. She and her husband, Rich, created the Challenge Day programs.

Dear Kimberly,

You will never know how much we appreciate all that you and the *Chicken Soup* organization have done for us. It never ceases to amaze me how angels show up when we least expect, but most need them. You couldn't have shown up at a better time.

I was nine months pregnant. My body felt so swollen, it seemed as if I might explode into a thousand pieces at any moment. Had it been a "normal" pregnancy, it might have been different. It wasn't, though. Eight-and-a-half months before, I became a surrogate mother for a very dear friend of mine, and the baby I was carrying was for her and her husband. I was overwhelmed with emotion. The tears that fell from my eyes were not just those of sadness, but of every feeling there is to be felt. I didn't know if I had the courage and strength to hand over a child that I had carried in my belly for what seemed like an eternity. To make matters even more complicated, I wasn't able to work. The teen workshops I lead with my husband were far too strenuous at thirty-six weeks pregnant. Challenge Days would have to wait. Our money began dwindling.

In a moment of total fear, I cried with my friend. I didn't know how we could possibly go on without working. My friend looked deep into my eyes. It was as if her words contained the wisdom of all the ages: "You are giving me the gift of a child. God will take care of you and support the work you do on this planet."

Not even an hour later, the phone rang. You told us you were sending a check on behalf of *Chicken Soup for the Teenage Soul*. A story about Challenge Day had appeared in your book, and you and your publisher, HCI, had chosen to make a very generous donation for the work we do to end pain and separation in young people's lives. My tears were now those of gratitude and joy. My body, for the first time in months, felt light and full of energy. The money was sent from the *Chicken Soup* organization . . . but I knew it came from God.

Two days later, I gave birth to the most beautiful baby boy I had ever seen—a gift for my friends. The amazing lesson of love I learned from letting go of that child and the generous contribution made from *Chicken Soup* helped to create a new beginning for our program. For years Challenge Day, a day of miracles, unity and forgiveness, had only been led by my husband and me. With the gift we received from *Chicken Soup for the Teenage Soul* and the renewed energy it brought us, we were able to train thirty new staff members, purchase new equipment, and extend the message of love and peace to thousands of youth and adults all over the world.

There is not a Challenge Day that goes by in which there aren't phenomenal healings that take place between people. We are proud to say there are literally hundreds of stories about the bridges that are built through our program, and we are so grateful to *Chicken Soup* for making some of those bridges happen.

With the help of *Chicken Soup for the Teenage Soul*, Challenge Day continues to blossom. It's people like you who make this world a better place. There are angels everywhere. Thank you for being one of ours on this journey to create a hate-free planet.

Our blessings and gratitude,
Yvonne and Rich St. John-Dutra

Helping Others

This program is profound and we are thrilled to be able to, once again, donate a portion of the proceeds of this book to it. We would also like to be able to see that the schools that need it the most don't get left out due to an inability to pay. Please contact us if you know of a school in great need of a Challenge Day program. We will choose two schools to receive the Challenge Day program and we will document it by publishing a story about the students' experiences both before and after the program. This story will appear in the upcoming *Chicken Soup for the Teenage Boy's Soul,* scheduled to be released Fall 2002.

If you would like to inquire about Challenge Day for your school or would like more information about the program, you may contact:

Challenge Day
P.O. Box 2208
Martinez, CA 94553
Phone: 925-957-0234
Web site: *www.challengeday.com*

A Day That Changed Us All

Dear Chicken Soup for the Teenage Soul,

On April 20, 1999, in a school across the country from mine, one of the biggest tragedies of my lifetime occurred: Two teenage boys entered Columbine High School in Littleton, Colorado, and killed thirteen people. The news devastated and scared me. The thought of a student coming into my own school and shooting people terrified me. I wasn't directly impacted by what happened at Columbine, but the tragedy affected me deeply.

I found solace in discussing the tragedy with my dad. He spent hours talking with me about my thoughts and feelings and he encouraged me, as he does so well, to think of ways that I could come to terms with what had happened. He asked me what I thought would make me feel better, and how we could show the students and those in the community that people around the world love them. I thought about it long and hard until I knew in my heart what I wanted to do. I realized I wanted to help the students—to give them something that could make them feel better and ease their pain, however slightly. I told my dad that I had found a great deal of comfort in reading the stories in *Chicken Soup for the Teenage Soul*. The stories in the book, I explained, helped me realize that we all have within us the power to overcome any obstacles. I wanted each of the students at Columbine to have a copy of *Chicken Soup for the Teenage Soul* to help them cope with this horribly painful ordeal.

My father immediately got on the phone to Health Communications, Inc., the publisher of the *Chicken Soup for the Soul* series, and explained to them that we wanted to purchase two thousand copies of *Chicken Soup for the Teenage Soul II* for the students at Columbine. The publisher was so receptive to the whole idea that they contacted Kimberly Kirberger, the coauthor, right away and told her what we wanted to do. She immediately called my house and said how deeply moved she was by what we were doing. She told us that she, the other coauthors of *Teenage Soul* and the publisher, without hesitation, had decided to match our purchase of two thousand books and donate two thousand *Chicken Soup for the Teenage Soul Journals* as well. I was ecstatic to say the least, not because I was proud of what I was doing, but for what these books would do for the Columbine students at such a traumatic time.

From that point on, everything else seemed to fall into place. So many people were willing to help out in any way they could. First, we needed a place to store the books once they arrived in Littleton, until they could be distributed. We were so fortunate to meet a very special woman from Media Play who was gracious enough to provide a storage place for the books. She made sure there were PTA members and other volunteers available to help stuff the books with letters written by myself and the *Chicken Soup for the Soul* team, and to help pass the books out to the students. And throughout the entire process, Darren Martin also helped in whatever ways he could.

I was not able to be in Littleton when the students received their books, but a few days later the letters and e-mail started pouring in. After reading all the amazing words about how happy they were to receive the books, I was able to picture in my mind their excitement on that day. I was overwhelmed by it all. It's difficult to find words to describe how incredible it was to receive all those letters, but it was a feeling I will treasure forever. I received letters not only from students of Columbine, but from parents and even a school bus driver. His was particularly touching because he told me that on the day the books were given out the mood of the students seemed to change. Faces brightened up just a bit. One morning with a bus full of students he looked in his rearview mirror and saw a sea of *Chicken Soup* books being read and teenagers beginning to regain those smiles they had before the shooting. He was so moved that he couldn't help but get choked up by what he saw.

Later, in September 1999, I received another phone call from Kimberly Kirberger. She was going to be in Colorado in October for book signings and was hoping my father and I could join her there. Without thinking twice about it, I told her we would make it.

We flew to Colorado to meet Kim and attend her book signing in Littleton. She was awesome! We got to know each other over dinner, and I don't think I have met a sweeter person than Kim. I was also able to meet a few of the Columbine students I had kept in contact with who were at the book signing. To be able to talk to them in person was something I really wanted to do and was important to me. They were extremely nice and outgoing—

their lives heading in the right direction now. It was the perfect culmination to everything that had happened.

Throughout the whole experience I became closer to those around me, including my family, friends and God. I received a tremendous amount of support from them and without it I would have had a really difficult time dealing with the Columbine shooting. One is never okay with something as tragic as this, but the love and support helped me tremendously, and I am very grateful for that.

I look at life differently now, knowing how precious it is and how quickly things can be turned upside down. I pray often that a tragedy such as Columbine never happens again.

Thank you so much *Chicken Soup for the Teenage Soul* for creating these amazing books and giving teenagers more hope, inspiration, love and encouragement.

God bless,
Jackie Morgenstern

[*Editors' Note:* The president of Health Communications, Inc., Peter Vegso, made the books available to Jackie at the publisher's cost. All of us involved with these books were deeply touched and inspired by Jackie and her father's kindness.]

The Violence Needs to Stop

Dear Chicken Soup for the Teenage Soul,

I am not going to start out this letter like most. I am writing for one reason and one reason only: to get my point across. I have held in so much for the past two years—so much frustration, so much pain and so much confusion. Nobody seems to care that teens today are dealing with so many tough issues in our communities and schools. I am a teen with strong opinions about the world we live in. I have ideas about the changes that need to be made, but I don't even know where to begin. I feel like I have no one to talk to about it all. No one seems to want to listen. So I'm not used to expressing myself. I've learned to stay quiet, and that hurts.

Two years ago, during the summer before ninth grade, I was attacked and beaten up by two girls I didn't even know. I was hanging out in my home-town with my boyfriend and some of my friends when these girls started verbally harassing us. Supposedly I "looked" at them wrong. Suddenly things escalated and they were yelling—and I was punched in the face over and over. It all happened so fast and I don't remember much, but I do remember looking at my friends and my boyfriend while I was being punched. They just stood there and didn't do a thing. These girls were tough and powerful in our high school, so my friends must have been scared. I hit the ground and blacked out. When I woke up I was in so much pain it was overwhelming. I had bruises all over me, and I couldn't move my jaw. I couldn't understand how this could have happened to me.

I had always led a relatively easy life. Until that day, violence or hatred did not even exist in my world. But I now know that they exist everywhere—and their long-term effects are powerful.

After the attack, I became depressed and cried all the time. All I wanted to do was stay in my room where I was safe. Ninth grade was painful. I felt like I had been stabbed in the back by most of my friends. Whenever I saw them at school, they just looked away. Fortunately, my best friend, Michelle, was there for me and helped me to get back on my feet in more ways than one.

I started to notice the problems all around me. I became sensitive to the remarks of others and started to notice that certain kids at my school were continually picked on and harassed by older, more powerful kids. Fights broke out all the time, and it seemed like there were certain kids who would wait for any excuse to beat somebody up. The verbal harassment was brutal. Nobody was safe from the taunting and teasing. We even had police officers at our school, but their presence did little good. They seemed to be more interested in chatting with the teachers than patrolling the hallways, where all the trouble was going on.

I started to dread going to school. My grades dropped dramatically. I couldn't talk to anyone about what I was experiencing so I became more and more quiet. My parents and I finally talked about what I should do, and we all decided that changing schools would be the best thing for me. We decided that I would attend an alternative, independent-study program.

That decision seemed to jumpstart something inside of me. By this point, I was sick and tired of feeling depressed all the time. So I made a decision. I decided to get well. I wanted to be whole again, to experience my life to the fullest. And to be joyful. I tried to make the most of what was left of my freshman year by meeting people and reaching out. My success in making new friends gave me more energy and helped me to stop crying and start laughing and smiling once again.

Now that I am a junior in high school, I have spent a lot of time thinking about my experience and what changes need to be made to make the world a safer place for children. Ending violence in our schools is something that is extremely close to my heart, for obvious reasons, and something that I am very committed to in my lifetime. It's not fair that people have to walk home from school and be afraid for their lives. It's not fair that young teens go to school feeling scared inside and feeling like they need to "watch their back" because their peers make them feel like they're two inches tall and don't amount to anything. It's not fair that teens are afraid to speak their mind for fear that others might get mad and try to "throw down" and pick a fight. The truth is, teen violence is everywhere, and kids don't feel safe even in my small town.

I have a lot more time on my hands than the average teen since I am in an independent-study program, so I have spent the last year writing letters to people who might be able to help—congresspeople, community leaders, teachers and now you. I am trying to get the word out to as many people as possible that things need to change—and they *can* change. It is possible. We all need to stand up and do something about it. Teens need role models, more counselors, conflict resolution skills and anger management classes. How hard would it be to take just an hour every other day to work on these issues in the schools? Kids need to come together and learn how to get along and try to make amends. We need a place where we can talk freely about our life, how our day is going, about our families and our friends, and about our feelings and emotions. We need help in coping with all our feelings and our fears. We need peer communication skills classes in our schools. We need community centers where teens can get together and help each other out. We need adults who can teach us how to help each other and teach us how to take a stand against violence and hatred.

Coincidentally, I happened to be watching UPN today and a show called *Teen Files* came on. It was about teen violence and was hosted by Leeza Gibbons. The show made an incredibly positive impression on me. I would do anything to be able to meet those courageous teens, to thank them for opening my eyes even further to the problem and for helping me to see ways to begin solving the problem. The solution is kindness. These teens are committed to leading a life of kindness and service to each other after all they have been through and seen. And that is what matters most—that we learn to treat each other with kindness and respect.

Two years ago I was brutally beaten by girls who didn't stop to think about the emotional and physical pain they were causing. I was left to feel hurt and alone. I am now committed to preventing my experience from happening to other teens. I am going to work to make all of our lives better, and I am starting with this letter. I want to make a difference, and I need help. Please help me to get my message out to other teens so that we may all begin to work together for safe streets and safe schools. Help me to be heard.

Sincerely,
Ashley Sims

Helping Others

I love this letter! As I was reading it, I couldn't help but talk out loud to it, repeating over and over, "Yes! Exactly!" For years, this is the message I have carried in my heart, and for decades my brother, Jack Canfield, has worked diligently to have schools be a place where self-esteem and kindness toward others are not only taught, but most highly valued. This year we started a project called Soup and Support for Teachers, where we provide at no cost *Chicken Soup* books and a teaching guide called *101 Ways to Use Chicken Soup in the Classroom: Teaching and Healing Students with Stories*. We have already received hundreds of letters from teachers saying that these stories work miracles in teaching compassion.

Also, the program mentioned, *Teen Files*, hosted by Leeza Gibbons, is the best thing I have seen regarding the challenges teens face and positive solutions. I highly recommend this show and hope you will watch it when you get a chance.

[*Editors' Note:* If you also want to make a difference in your community and work toward safer streets and schools, here are some resources that we have found to be both useful and inspiring:

Be a Global Force of One! 202 Common Sense, Portable and Human Ways to Restore Our Communities, Our Schools and Ourselves. *John T. Boal, PacRim Publishing, March 1998.*

Can Students End School Violence? Solutions from America's Youth. *Jason Ryan Dorsey, Archstone Press, LLC, November 1999.*]

A Teacher's Dream

Dear Chicken Soup for the Teenage Soul,

Teachers are constantly searching for ways to motivate today's teens to read and write, especially the most reluctant students who are being held accountable for passing state-mandated tests. For years I encouraged students to read and write for publication, but I think they always felt that this "old-lady English teacher" was just trying to con them into more work. But now that my students' pieces have appeared in national publications and in your latest volume of *Chicken Soup for the Teenage Soul*, I feel compelled to share my story of success with others and admit that all the credit is due to your *Chicken Soup for the Teenage Soul* series.

My own introduction to the stories occurred during an airline flight overseas. I read the first volume of *Chicken Soup for the Teenage Soul* in hopes of finding a story or two I could use in my "slow learner" class that year. By the time I reached the Frankfurt airport, tears were flowing, prompting inquiring looks from nearby seatmates, and I knew I had hit "pay dirt." If the stories affected me as they did, then certainly they would engage students in the classes most teachers dread to instruct. But I also knew that: (1) I would not receive school funds to purchase copies for the students as most funds were then being spent on computers, (2) I could not ditto enough copies on a regular basis without the "keeper" of the copy machine vehemently protesting, and (3) school committees had to approve all textbooks, but with "slow learners" good materials are so scarce that anything used to supplement instruction is most appreciated, especially if the teachers pay for them.

Nationwide, teachers spend approximately $300–$500 of their own money each year on materials, most of which is used to help them survive on a day-to-day basis. For me, with the three classes of "slow learners" I was scheduled to teach in the fall, every dime I spent on a class set of *Chicken Soup for the Teenage Soul* would be well worth it. So, armed with my school's tax number and a request for the 10 percent educator's discount, I asked the local Crown bookstore to order thirty-five copies. Then, I sat down with my own copy of the book to organize the stories so that they could be used as motivators for writing assignments.

Fortunately, the books arrived a week after school began, and I chose a few of my favorite stories to read in class. I had the students discuss their impact, and we studied the writers' style, point of view, diction and voice before embarking on the first composition assignment. What amazed me is that these "reluctant students" read with such intensity and gave such rapt attention to the stories that I, as the teacher, could have been a thousand miles away. Some even sat in my classroom during their lunch periods to read a story someone else had recommended. Admittedly, a few copies were stolen, so I made the remaining copies as ugly as possible, putting my name on the binding and stamping the school's name throughout. Each day in class, a student would come to the front of the room to read a story while sitting in the "reader's chair" because reading aloud to others is a skill not often practiced by the "reluctant reader." Then, we would read the short biography of the author found in the back of the book, and students would write their reaction to the story, its "lesson" or "moral," and ideas for compositions of their own in a reading journal.

What followed was magic. Students loved the quotes that prefaced each story and kept their own lists of favorite quotes that they had heard, read or simply enjoyed, and eventually would use when they wrote their own pieces. If Mick Jagger could write, "It's all right letting yourself go, as long as you can get yourself back," surely they, too, could create or collect their own favorite quotes. Admittedly, some were off-color, but I did not censor their reading journals. Instead, I encouraged them to write appropriately and to remember that they had to be inclusive and appeal to all ages, groups and political persuasions if getting published was their ultimate goal.

Then we added vocabulary words from the book in preparation for the SATs—words like "knaves" in Kipling's "If"; "premonition" from "The Premonition" by Bruce Burch, which they associated with "omens"; and "inconsequential" from "Lilacs Bloom Every Spring." When we discovered that one of the writers in *Chicken Soup for the Teenage Soul* lived near us in Columbia, Maryland, we invited Amanda Dykstra to our classes to read and discuss her poem, "The Girl Next Door." Amanda was beautiful, articulate and passionate in her reading, and she told students that her life had dramatically changed since the publication of her poem. She spoke of her book-signings, the accolades and letters she had received, and the fame her one-page poem had brought her. Needless to say, students were incredulous that a girl her age was a nationally "published author."

Students were also impressed that celebrities they knew and admired had written stories for the book—stars like Bill Cosby, Jennifer Love Hewitt and actor Clifton Davis. The students decided to write their own favorite rock stars, sports heroes and political figures, and suggested to them that they, too, submit stories to the editors of *Chicken Soup* in hopes that you would eventually compile a celebrity version of your series.

After reading the stories in the "On Family" chapter, the students decided to write tributes and letters of thanks to their own parents that could be mailed to them and then offered to local newspapers for publication to celebrate Mother's Day, Father's Day and Grandparents' Day. Needless to say, the reaction from parents was overwhelming. Most admitted that they were emotionally moved by their child's thoughts and memories of them. Some pieces were sent to the editor of *Senior Edition, U.S.A.* in Boulder, Colorado, and upon publication, she sent the student-authors small royalty checks. By then, students were encouraging their own parents to write and submit their stories to *Chicken Soup*. Ninth-grader Jessica Parsons persuaded her father to write about his memory of Jessica's birth and submit it. At a fall PTA meeting, the principal announced that Mr. Parsons' story was under consideration for your next volume on parenting.

By then, students were writing more anecdotal detail, were proofreading and editing more before submitting their stories, and were coercing their parents to write tributes to them and other narratives and poems as well. The parents sent their signed and sealed tributes to their children to me, and on the last day of school in June, the students opened and read their parents' tributes to them. I overheard one student say, "I never knew my parents felt that way about me." None of us left class that day with a dry eye, and some have forwarded their parents' work to your editorial staff. By now, not only the reluctant students were profiting from the unit, but my gifted and talented students and honors classes were also taking part. Parents admitted that, for the first time, they felt part of their child's writing program.

Another benefit of using your book in class is that discussions were elevated to considering the positive effects of using dialogue, topic sentences and anecdotal detail in student written work that made the pieces more publishable. The sections "On Love and Kindness" and "Making a Difference" spurred many students to remember and write of their volunteer efforts for former President George Bush's 1,000 Points of Light Foundation's magazine. When *Chicken Soup for the Teenage Soul II* was released, I bought another class set, and students began to compare and argue over which volume contained the best stories. They even compiled their favorites and wrote reviews of the stories for the PTA newsletter. In my "Losing Our Childhood" unit, Eva Burke's "The Days of Cardboard Boxes" was their favorite; in the "Sports" unit, Marsha Arons's "The Cheerleader" touched a nerve for girls, while "From Crutches to a World-Class Runner" appealed mostly to boys.

One day, coincidentally on National Teacher Appreciation Day, we read Diana L. Chapman's "Mrs. Virginia DeView, Where Are You?" that ends with the line, "Perhaps you [the reader] can thank her [your favorite teacher] before it's too late." As a result of that story, the students suggested they write letters of appreciation to their favorite teachers. The response was incredible. Some teachers, who by this point resided in nursing homes, called or wrote to confess, "This is the first time I have ever received a thank-you from a former student, and it brought tears to my eyes." What students were learning was the power of the written word and the effects their writing could have on real

people, not only their old-lady English teacher—
something they had never before realized. In addi-
tion, during our "Dating and Relationships" unit
and following the reading of Mary Jane West-
Delgado's "My First Kiss and Then Some," they each
wrote of their own first kiss, and we mailed some
of the best to the *Washington Post* in celebration of
upcoming Valentine's Day. Imagine their surprise
and delight when some were published, reaching
a national readership! Students were learning the
value of writing for a larger audience beyond their
peers, their parents and their teacher.

Each time I asked the students to talk about how
far they had come in their reading and their ability
to discuss meaningful pieces and write publishable
short stories, they admitted that it was because
Chicken Soup for the Teenage Soul dealt with subjects they couldn't openly discuss in other classes.
Somehow, connecting those "taboo subjects" to
the literature component of my English class made
the subjects palatable to the administration, and
we've never been reprimanded for going "outside
the prescribed curriculum." Granted that homosex-
uality, diversity, prejudice, sexuality, patriotism, religion, suicide, drug use, abuse, loneliness and
discrimination are hot topics, but when your students are reading and writing like never before and

parents see their child's name in print, no one is going to argue with success.

What this unit showed me is that if a teacher finds the right selections of literature, miracles do occur. I wasn't asking them to read and react to Whitman's *Leaves of Grass*, but instead to modern stories that pulled their heartstrings, spoke their language, grabbed their attention, and demonstrated that even teen writers can engage a national reading public. Because of their success, I often get asked to share my unit with other teachers at the National Council of Teachers of English conventions. It remains to be seen if this unit increases students' test scores on state assessments, but I can tell you that my school's reputation for quality writing has reached far and wide. In fact, my student, Sydney Fox, whose family has worked for years with the homeless and destitute in our area, wrote of a budding teen friendship that went sour in a story titled "Terri Jackson." The day she read the story to the class two years ago, I knew it was powerful enough to be included in *Chicken Soup for the Teenage Soul III* and, fortunately, your editors agreed. A few months ago, following the release of *Teen III*, Sydney was featured in the local newspapers, appeared on TV and completed two book-signing parties—one at a local Barnes and Noble store and another at our high school.

Suddenly, the dream of being published in a national bestselling book became a realistic goal for our students.

Last winter, fifteen of our seniors published their own anthology of short stories entitled *Icarus Rising*, which was partly funded by a Teaching Tolerance grant from the Southern Poverty Law Center in Montgomery, Alabama. The small volume has been so popular in our area that a local university made it required reading for their incoming freshmen at the school's orientation. This little red paperback gives teachers and parents hope that today's students are capable of soaring to new heights in reading, writing and publishing.

After years spent encouraging students to write, it is beyond words how proud I feel to see their names in print. At long last I will retire this fall because I feel I've been somewhat a success by getting at least one student published in your series. May your books never end because we English teachers realize their magic. Thank you for helping make dreams come true.

Sincerely,
Kathy A. Megyeri

P.S. This year the unexpected happened, and it made me more mindful of the importance of writing tributes as part of our *Chicken Soup for the*

Teenage Soul unit. Upon my return from winter break, I received this letter from a student's father.

> Christopher's mother passed away unexpectedly in her sleep on Christmas Eve. Chris and I are obviously devastated by the loss of his mother and my wife of twenty-seven years. I would like to thank you in advance for taking into account his feelings during this most difficult time. The tribute that Chris wrote to his mom as your class assignment on December 21, just four days before her death, so moved her that she wrote a tribute back to him. At her funeral service this past Tuesday, the minister read both Chris's tribute to his mom and her tribute back to him. This was a very moving moment for me, and I thank you for assigning this. Little did I know it would be needed so soon.

Helping Others

On behalf of Kathy Megyeri, we are donating books in her name to the school from which Ms. Megyeri retired this year. After many years of dedicated service as an English teacher at Sherwood High School, it is hoped that her creative and inspired teaching methods will live on in the hearts of the teachers who remain and continue to motivate young writers and readers for years to come. It is largely due to her letter that we formed the program "Soup and Support for Teachers" and the teaching guide called *101 Ways to Use Chicken Soup in the Classroom: Teaching and Healing Students with Stories.*

Dusty Sentiments

[*Editors' Note:* We called Amanda Dykstra because we thought it would be interesting to hear about her experience with Ms. Megyeri's class.]

Dear Chicken Soup for the Teenage Soul,

I was on the second-to-last page of Myla Goldberg's *Bee Season* when my phone rang last week. I was so engrossed in it that I heard the telephone ring and, confusing it for the oven timer, raced to the kitchen to check on the muffins I was making for a weekend road trip. Imagine my confusion when the muffins were still soupy and the "timer" wouldn't stop ringing when I opened the oven door. Fortunately, I made it to the phone before the answering machine picked up.

Obviously, your call caught me off-guard—not only

because it woke me from my novel-induced trance, but also because I'd lost touch with you since I moved to Michigan three years ago, the summer after the debut of *Chicken Soup for the Teenage Soul*. (My e-mail address changed along with my phone number and street address, which is why many *Chicken Soup* fans who wrote to me did not receive replies. Sorry!) So, the phone call was a real blast from my past, as well as a pleasant surprise.

You asked for an update about me. Well, my life is about to get relatively exciting. I graduated from West Ottawa High School in June and will start my freshman year at Hope College later this month. (Is it *really* just three weeks away?) I've spent a fair amount of time sorting through the contents of closets, drawers and my under-the-bed stash, deciding what will accompany me to my new room in Gilmore Hall and what will stay home. But I frequently get sidetracked—I'm a sentimental person, not to mention a pack rat, and I often run across letters, journals and other keepsakes that are loaded with history. Last week, I found a shoe box in my closet that was bulging with artifacts of my fifteenth year: dried red rose petals from a corsage, an inch-thick stack of printouts of e-mails, even an unopened can of potted meat, the expiration date a distant memory. I spent the whole afternoon stretched out on the rug in my room, examining each relic and reliving the story it represented. Scattered at the bottom of the box were fourteen index cards covered in my own black scrawls. I couldn't make any sense of them until I found the card marked with a numeral 1 in the upper left-hand corner, across the top of which I'd scribbled "SHERWOOD SPIEL."

Those index cards served as my lifeline for the day in October 1997 that I spent with Ms. Megyeri's English classes at Sherwood High School. Ms. Megyeri wrote to me soon after *Chicken Soup for the Teenage Soul* was published, explaining that her freshmen had been reading selections from the book in class and modeling their own anecdotes after them. She invited me to speak to her classes about the experience of having my work—"The Girl Next Door"*—published. *What a neat idea,* I thought, *to use this book to get teenagers excited about writing!* I accepted the invitation without a second thought.

Then I started to panic. I'm no stranger to audiences; between music and drama, I've spent a fair amount of time performing. But those mediums usually involve dark auditoriums that obscure spectators' faces and stage lights that blind me anyway. When I can see people's faces, and when I'm not

---

* *"The Girl Next Door," by Amanda Dykstra,* Chicken Soup for the Teenage Soul, *pp. 276–278.*

viewing them from the safety of the stage, it's another matter. I've always been the kind of kid who gets tongue-tied during oral reports, or any other situation in which I have to play "teacher." Public speaking really doesn't come naturally to me.

So I wrote myself a script of sorts, one that provided answers to the questions I'd frequently been asked by new classmates and reporters for local newspapers: I'd posted "The Girl Next Door" in a teen writers' forum, where it had been found by Kimberly Kirberger. Yes, I had drawn on personal experience to write it. I wanted to have a career as a writer. The way to improve the quality of one's writing was to try to write every day.

Now, I'm startled by the confidence with which I lumped all of those statements into the category of Indisputable Truths, especially since I've been asking myself the corresponding questions quite often lately: How on earth did I manage to publish my work? Where did I find my inspiration? What do I want to do with the rest of my life? And how can I nurture this little talent of mine so that it grows, bears fruit and puts food on my table?

Part of me dismisses my fifteen-year-old self as an idealistic naif. Another part envies her confidence, and still another thinks her assertions just might have merit—that I could, perhaps, learn a lot from her.

Earlier this summer, my flute teacher suggested that I take on some students of my own. "You're ready," she said, "and teaching is a great way to reinforce what you already know. You'll be surprised at what you can learn from your students."

This wisdom isn't limited to the realm of instruction in music, or even to teaching in a classroom, but to any person who has ever shared an insight or a bit of advice. It also sums up my *Chicken Soup* experience rather neatly. As the author of "The Girl Next Door," I taught by the sharing of insight. The lesson is open-ended—I can only express the regret I feel for my neighbor. I can't tell the reader how to feel. But I am accountable for the feelings I've expressed.

Also, as I stood before Ms. Megyeri's students nearly three years ago, I assumed the role of a teacher by sharing my experience. I was asked many intelligent questions; I can't know whether the answers I provided were helpful to the bright people who asked them, but I do know that, for me, they served as a reaffirmation of what I knew to be true. And there was one student in particular from whom I learned a great deal—that day, I received a sneak preview of Sydney Fox's "Terri Jackson." I was sure I'd see it in print in a future edition of *Chicken Soup for the Teenage Soul*.

Anyway, as I sat on the floor of my room—surrounded by piles of what an impartial observer would call "junk"—I paper-clipped those fourteen index cards together and placed them back in the shoebox. I felt sincere gratitude for the reminder of the confidence I had when I was fifteen, which, I must admit, has been rattled somewhat by my current transition. Maybe I *will* end up being a writer. If not, perhaps there's room in this world for another English teacher.

Yours,

Amanda Anne-Marie Dykstra

More Chicken Soup?

Many of the letters, stories and poems that you have read in this book were submitted by readers like you who have read *Chicken Soup for the Teenage Soul* and the other *Chicken Soup for the Soul* books. In the future, we are planning to publish *Chicken Soup for the Teenage Soul IV*, *Chicken Soup for the Teenage Soul on Tough Stuff*, *Chicken Soup for the Teenage Boy's Soul* and *Chicken Soup for the Teenage Christian Soul*. We would love to have you contribute a story, poem or letter to one of these future books.

This may be a story you write yourself, or one you clip out of your school newspaper, local newspaper, church bulletin or a magazine. It might be something you read in a book or find on the Internet. It could also be a favorite poem, quotation or cartoon you have saved. Please also send along as much information as you know about where it came from.

Just send a copy of your stories or other pieces to us at this address:

Chicken Soup for the Teenage Soul
P.O. Box 936
Pacific Palisades, CA 90272
e-mail: *stories@iam4teens.com*
Web site: *www.iam4teens.com*

Who Is Jack Canfield?

Jack Canfield is a best-selling author and one of America's leading experts in the development of human potential. He is both a dynamic and entertaining speaker and a highly sought-after trainer with a wonderful ability to inform and inspire audiences to open their hearts, love more openly and boldly pursue their dreams.

Jack spent his teenage years growing up in Martins Ferry, Ohio, and Wheeling, West Virginia, with his sister Kimberly (Kirberger) and his two brothers, Rick and Taylor. The whole family has spent most of their professional careers dedicated to educating, counseling and empowering teens. Jack admits to being shy and lacking self-confidence in high school, but through a lot of hard work he earned letters in three sports and graduated third in his class.

After graduating college, Jack taught high school in the inner city of Chicago and in Iowa. In recent years, Jack has expanded this to include adults in both educational and corporate settings.

He is the author and narrator of several bestselling audio- and videocassette programs. He is a regularly consulted expert for radio and television broadcasts and has published twenty-five books—all bestsellers within their categories—including more than twenty *Chicken Soup for the Soul* books, *The Aladdin Factor, Heart at Work, 100 Ways to Build Self-Concept in the Classroom* and *Dare to Win.*

Jack addresses over one hundred groups each year. His clients include professional associations, school districts, government agencies, churches and corporations in all fifty states.

Jack conducts an annual eight-day Training of Trainers program in the areas of building self-esteem and achieving peak performance. It attracts educators, counselors, parenting trainers, corporate trainers, professional speakers, ministers and others interested in developing their speaking and seminar-leading skills in these areas.

For further information about Jack's books, tapes and trainings, or to schedule him for a presentation, please contact:

The Canfield Training Group
P.O. Box 30880 • Santa Barbara, CA 93130
phone: 800-237-8336 • fax: 805-563-2945
e-mail: *speaking@canfieldgroup.com*
Web site: *www.chickensoup.com*

Who Is Mark Victor Hansen?

Mark Victor Hansen is a professional speaker who, in the last twenty years, has made over four thousand presentations to more than two million people in thirty-three countries. His presentations cover sales excellence and strategies; personal empowerment and development; and how to triple your income and double your time off.

Mark has spent a lifetime dedicated to his mission of making a profound and positive difference in people's lives. Throughout his career, he has inspired hundreds of thousands of people to create a more powerful and purposeful future for themselves while stimulating the sale of billions of dollars worth of goods and services.

Mark is a prolific writer and has authored *Future Diary, How to Achieve Total Prosperity* and *The Miracle of Tithing*. He is the coauthor of the *Chicken Soup for the Soul* series, *Dare to Win* and *The Aladdin Factor* (all with Jack Canfield) and *The Master Motivator* (with Joe Batten).

Mark has also produced a complete library of personal empowerment audio- and videocassette programs that have enabled his listeners to recognize and better use their innate abilities in their business and personal lives. His message has made him a popular television and radio personality with appearances on ABC, NBC, CBS, HBO, PBS, QVC and CNN.

He has also appeared on the cover of numerous magazines, including *Success, Entrepreneur* and *Changes*.

Mark is a big man with a heart and a spirit to match—an inspiration to all who seek to better themselves.

For further information about Mark, please contact:

Mark Victor Hansen & Associates
P.O. Box 7665
Newport Beach, CA 92658
phone: 949-759-9304 or 800-433-2314
fax: 949-722-6912
Web site: *www.chickensoup.com*

Who Is Kimberly Kirberger?

Kimberly is an advocate for teens, a writer for teens, a mother of a teen, and a friend and confidante to the many teens in her life. She is committed to bettering the lives of teens around the globe through her books and the outreach she does for teens on behalf of her organization, Inspiration and Motivation for Teens, Inc.

Kim's love for teens was first expressed globally with the publication of the bestselling *Chicken Soup for the Teenage Soul*. This book was a true labor of love for Kim, and the result of years of friendship and research with teens from whom she learned what really matters. After the success of the first *Teenage Soul* book, and the outpouring of hundreds and thousands of letters and submissions from teens around the world, Kim went on to coauthor the *New York Times* #1 bestsellers *Chicken Soup for the Teenage Soul II* and *Chicken Soup for the Teenage Soul III, Chicken Soup for the Teenage Soul Journal* and *Chicken Soup for the College Soul*. Kim's empathic understanding of the issues affecting parents led her to coauthor the recent release *Chicken Soup for the Parent's Soul*.

In October 1999, the first book in Kim's *Teen Love* series was released. *Teen Love: On Relationships* has since become a *New York Times* bestseller. Her friendship and collaboration with Colin Mortensen of MTV's *Real World Hawaii* produced the much-loved *Teen Love: A Journal on Relationships* and *Teen Love: On Friendship*. She recently released *Teen Love: A Journal on Friendship*.

Kim lives in Southern California with her husband, John, and son, Jesse. When she is not reading letters she gets from teens, she is offering them support and encouragement in the forums on her Web site, *www.iam4teens.com*. She also enjoys nurturing her family, listening to her son's band and hanging out with her friends.

Kimberly and Colin have been speaking at high schools and middle schools, and have developed a much sought-after program for teens.

For information or to schedule Kim and Colin for a presentation, contact:

I.A.M. for Teens, Inc.
P.O. Box 936
Pacific Palisades, CA 90272
e-mail for stories: *stories@iam4teens.com*
e-mail for letters and feedback: *kim@iam4teens.com*
Web site: *www.iam4teens.com*

Contributors

Lizzie A. Agra is currently a student at Rio Linda High School in Sacramento, California. Writing is just a pastime for her, but she's honored to have this opportunity to share her story with the world. She sends her love to all those people in her life who have made her the person that she is. She sends all the readers her sincere regards. Remember, "Life doesn't have to be perfect to be wonderful."

Melinda Allen is a seventeen-year-old senior in Goffstown, New Hampshire. She holds a black belt in American Kenpo Karate and currently works as a karate instructor. Melinda is also an avid snowboarder and plans to continue both hobbies at Assumption College in the fall.

Katie Benson is a student at Central High School in Little Rock, Arkansas. She likes to play soccer, snow ski and spend time with her friends. Katie can be reached by e-mail at *Katrisha@hotmail.com*.

Rachel N. Bentley is one of eight adopted/permanent foster/birth sisters. She has spent over fifteen years helping her family minister to over forty foster kids, primarily troubled teen girls. Now in her twenties and married, Rachel still ministers to teenagers and is very outspoken on pro-family issues. She is also very involved in music and enjoys her eleven (so far!) nieces and nephews. She can be reached at *a2jc4life@yahoo.com*.

Andrea Blake is a college student currently pursuing a degree in social work. She has been working with at-risk youth in her community for two years. She has a strong dedication to empowering America's youth for the future. Andrea helped create and write a teen resource guide for 30,000 area high-school students. She has also been a member of the National Network for Youth for two years. You can reach her by e-mail at *arb@columus.rr.com*.

Michelle Bouchard is a full-time university student in Canada. She aspires to become a French immersion teacher. For the meantime, she is happy being young and independent. She would like to dedicate her writing to everyone who ever felt that there was something emotionally or physically "wrong" with themselves: You are not alone. Michelle can be reached by e-mail at *Mitch097@hotmail.com* or by mail at Box 228, Knutsford, British Columbia, Canada, V0E 2A0.

Alicia M. Boxler is a senior in high school, who enjoys hanging out with her friends, drawing, writing, playing the flute, and listening to Third Eye Blind and Blink 182. This story is dedicated to her best friends, Lisa, Erin, Ellie, and Danielle, who always proved that laughter is the best medicine. Alicia can be reached through e-mail at *AlternaG15@aol.com*.

Cassandra Brady is currently a college student in Broken Arrow, Oklahoma. She enjoys writing for her own pleasure, but aspires to become a published poet in the future. This letter is dedicated to her close friend, Kella. She can be reached by e-mail at *Kass5P@hotmail.com*.

Kelsey Brunone is a fourteen-year-old from Pennsylvania. She has enjoyed writing her entire life and had two poems published when she was thirteen—one in an anthology of poetry and the other in *WordDance*, (a children's literary magazine). Kelsey wrote this letter when she was in the seventh grade.

Natalie Cabrera is a freshman in college majoring in communications. She has been a member of the Girl Scouts for twelve years and hopes to continue her involvement in the community. She hopes the Yellow Ribbon Program will inspire her and move others as she was by the powerful message it speaks. She can be reached by e-mail at *Nat37@aol.com*.

Kelsey Cameron is a second-year kinesiology student at Dalhousie University in Halifax, NS. She is a '98 recipient of the Canadian Merit Scholarship, which has given her much support and motivation. When she is not busy with her role as a residence assistant, she's training or teaching karate. Kelsey loves life and looks forward to one day fulfilling her dreams of becoming a doctor. She can be reached by e-mail at *klcamero@is2.dal.ca*.

Melanie Campbell—born, raised and educated throughout Asia—continues to write about the hardships others must endure due to poverty, corruption and a lack of love. A strong believer in human rights advocacy and philanthropy, her writing is dedicated to all people who fight to survive in a world where "innocence is lost too fast to understand and poverty captures millions unwilling to let go."

Jiseon Choi is fourteen years old and is a high-school student in Santa Maria, California. She leads a bright and active life, and enjoys playing volleyball, talking on the phone, shopping, listening to music and playing the piano. This is her first story to be published, and she would like to thank God for all the wonderful blessings he has bestowed upon her.

Cheryl L. Costello-Forshey is a freelance writer and poet. Her poetry can be found in *A 4th Course of Chicken Soup for the Soul, A 5th Portion of Chicken Soup for the Soul, Chicken Soup for the Teenage Soul II* and *III, Chicken Soup for the College Soul, Chicken Soup for the Parent's Soul, Stories for a Teen's Heart* and *Stories for a Faithful Heart*. Cheryl can be reached by e-mail at *costello-forshey@1st.net*.

Mary Davis lives in Southern California and is a part of the class of 2002 at her high school. She enjoys spending time with her friends and family. She wrote "A Loving Change" during her freshman year and is very glad to be sharing it with you. She would like to thank all of the people who have been there for her and have supported her (you know who you are!). She can be reached by e-mail at *PinkAnGel@aol.com*.

Lissa Desjardins is a junior in high school in New Brunswick, Canada. She hopes to pursue a career in fashion design. She has enjoyed doing figure skating for a number of years and plans to continue. This is Lissa's first published work. She can be reached by e-mail at *lissa_d69@hotmail.com*.

Corey Dweck is the author of *iam4teens.com*'s "Little Voice" column. His writing has appeared in such publications as *MH-18, Real Kids Real Adventures #12,* and *The Market Guide for Young Writers, 6th Edition.* He aspires and perspires to have his own book published. You can reach him by e-mail at *dweck@ptdprolog.net.*

Deena Ecker is currently a student at Brandeis University. She has been a Girl Scout since she was five. She especially enjoyed her last year with her troop planning the Yellow Ribbon Program, making lists and eating peanut M&M's. Deena enjoys reading, writing, acting and white-water river rafting with her family. She is more than overwhelmed with the fact that she was able to help so many people. Deena can be reached at *pezgirl014@hotmail.com*.

Katie Ecker is a student in South St. Paul, Minnesota. When she is older she would like to become a psychologist. When she was younger she would dream of being an author. She can be reached at *KTE3434@aol.com*.

Dale and **Dar Emme** started the Yellow Ribbon Suicide Prevention Program after losing their youngest son, Mike, seventeen, to suicide in 1994 and are dedicated to saving lives. They are in high demand giving presentations, workshops and in-services to youth, parents, teachers, staff, churches and communities across America and internationally.

Emily Ferry is a nineteen-year-old college student at Moorpark Junior College. She plans to transfer to CSUN to get her B.A. in Child Psychology. In her spare time she wants to write, sing for her brother's band, run her own restaurant and start a horseback-riding school. Although all of these might seem like a far-off, impossible fantasy she plans to try to do them all and hopes that a few of them will happen.

Michele Fiorentini is a freshman college student at the University of Illinois Urbana/Champaign. She is currently studying to be an accountant. Michele has been writing for a long time, though strictly for her own enjoyment. This is her first published work. She dedicates this story to those people who have been teased.

F.J.M. is a first-year student at the University of Toronto, where she is studying Physical and Health Education and Science. She loves swimming, camping, writing and leadership activities, and hopes to one day open her own clinic to help athletes with eating disorders. She wants to thank her friends for their love, laughs and smiles, and can't wait to cross Canada on bike! Her writing is dedicated with love forever to A.G. and her mom.

Adam Heise is a student at the University of Illinois at Urbana/Champaign. He is a born-again Christian who grew up in Lombard, Illinois. He is an avid outdoorsman, and aspires to be a high-school science teacher. He also enjoys music and reading when he's not busy with schoolwork. He welcomes any questions or comments about alopecia areata. He can be reached by e-mail at *adamheise@hotmail.com*.

Wanda Marie Goh Jen Jen is a nineteen-year-old freshman in Monash University Sunway Malaysia, where she is currently pursuing a degree in Business and Commerce. She was the editor of the ECHO, Sunway College's Editorial Board and has written for numerous Malaysian student publications. She enjoys writing poetry, art, traveling, dancing and hanging out with her friends. She can be reached by e-mail at *wanda@tm.net.my* or you can visit her Web site at *www.justfree.com/angelsofsoleil/jen.html*.

Jackie Johnstone is a grade twelve honors student at Preston High School in Cambridge, Ontario, Canada. She enjoys hanging out with friends, writing and listening to music in her spare time. Her letter is dedicated to all of her incredible friends—life wouldn't be the same without them. She can be reached by e-mail at *Air234ever@hotmail.com*.

Karen is a fifteen-year-old high-school student who lives in Toronto, Ontario. She loves to draw, listen to music and spend time with her friends. Her letter is dedicated to a special friend.

Kirsti Kay was born in South Africa in 1983. Her father was an accountant and her mother is a teacher. She has a sister four years older than her. Her father died three days after her thirteenth birthday. She was homeschooled from grade eleven until she graduated at the end of 2000. She loves outdoor life. She has her own horse and rides as often as possible.

Heather Klassen is from Edmonds, Washington, and writes for children and teenagers. She has had two picture books published and over one hundred stories appear in magazines. She can be reached by e-mail at *tressen60@cs.com*.

Rebecca Kross is a student at Lehigh University in Pennsylvania. She is currently in her junior year and is majoring in French and International Careers. She has continued her study of music, playing the French horn for the Philharmonic Orchestra at her university. She would like to thank her mother for her constant love and encouragement. She can be reached at *Beccabec5@aol.com*.

Kari J. Lee attended Purdue University (B.A. '93) and Ball State University (M.A. '95, M.A. '98). She is a health education and social skills teacher for the Youth Opportunity Center and the Muncie Community Schools. She is currently working towards her doctorate degree and lives with her Chihuahua named Beani. She wrote this letter in honor of her students.

Gary LeRoux is twenty-five years old and lives in Louisiana. He is interested in reading and writing about juvenile issues. His writing skills mainly include letters and poetry concerning juvenile justice. He can be reached at P.O. Box 2103, Reserve, LA 70084.

Jennifer Lirette is a thirteen-year-old from Moncton, New Brunswick, Canada. She is a serious student and enjoys writing, reading, listening to music, playing badminton, surfing the Internet and being involved with her school. She can be reached by e-mail at *Kitty1_2@hotmail.com*.

Kim Lowery is a fifteen-year-old freshman. She loves animals and playing softball with her friends Chelsea and Andrea. She likes giving advice to her friends, as well as receiving it. She has learned so much from her mistakes and hopes to help others make the right decisions. After high school she wants to attend college. She greatly appreciates the help and support from her friends and family, especially her mother. She can be reached by e-mail at *TigBittiez15@aol.com*.

Ashley Lusk is currently a member of the class of 2002 at F-C High School in Collinsville, Virginia. She enjoys reading, writing, drama and theater, Girl Scouts and the National Beta Club. She someday hopes to be a journalist, an actress or a teacher for the hearing impaired. She dedicates this to everyone who needs a fighting chance and to her mother. You can reach her by e-mail at *Drama_gal02@yahoo.com*.

Lauren Mark is currently a senior at Catholic Memorial High School in Waukesha, Wisconsin. She loves jazz and modern dance, performing in musical theater with her friends, and little children. She loves to pour her emotions into her writing, whether it's in letters to her friends or to *Chicken Soup for the Soul*.

Jennifer Martin is a writer and educator living in Roseville, California. She is listed in *Who's Who Among American Teachers, 1998*. She has also hosted and produced local television programs as well as national shows on the Travel Network. She can be reached by e-mail at *bgardner@calweb.com*.

Paula McDonald has sold over a million copies of her books on relationships and gone on to win numerous awards worldwide as a columnist, inspirational feature writer and photojournalist. She lives on the beach in Rosarito, Mexico. She can be contacted in the United States by writing PMB 724, 416 W. San Ysidro Blvd., Ste. L, San Ysidro, CA 92173 or by e-mailing *eieiho@compuserve.com*.

Crystal McHargue is currently between life paths: a job or college. This is her first published piece, which is exciting for an aspiring writer. She lives in Canada, but plans to move to the United States in the future.

Lisa McKinney is a beauty consultant in Spokane, Washington. She is a college student studying Criminal Justice at Spokane Falls. She would like to thank her mom for all her support. She can be reached by e-mail at *Caligodess@aol.com*.

Kathy A. Megyeri has taught high-school English for thirty-four years. She is most proud of her students who have been published, one in particular in *Chicken Soup for the Teenage Soul III*. She, too, writes a monthly column on education concerns and is frequently a guest speaker on "infusing service-learning into the Language Arts curriculum." She can be reached by e-mail at *Megyeri@juno.com*.

Kerri Meulemans attends a Big Ten University. She intends to pursue a dual major in the fields of Journalism and Public Relations after finding great interest in serving as a creative editor for her high-school newspaper. She aspires to eventually obtain a career working for a newspaper, magazine or publishing company. She can be reached by e-mail at *meuleman@athenet.net*.

Emily R. Monfort is a sophomore at South Eugene High School and International High School in Eugene, Oregon. She has never been published, but writing stories and poetry is one of her many hobbies. She plays soccer for her school, loves to snowboard, wakeboard and white-water raft with her family. She loves to read and, after finishing *Chicken Soup for the Teenage Soul*, she felt motivated to send in a story about a life experience that could be inspiring to others.

Rachel A. Morgan is a high-school sophomore in California. She enjoys writing political commentaries, and she has been published in several newspapers and magazines. Rachel is a strong advocate for children with disabilities, and she enjoys playing flute and piccolo. She can be reached via e-mail at *us780683@pacbell.net*.

Jackie Morgenstern is a junior at McDowell High School in Erie, Pennsylvania. She is involved in many events at her church, such as her youth group, praise band, choir and her school basketball team. Jackie loves helping people and plans to go to college in the future. She can be reached by e-mail at *Sweet2846@aol.com*.

Laura Motyka is currently a college freshman. She plans on majoring in psychology and eventually obtaining a Ph.D. in neuropsychology. Writing is one of Laura's favorite pastimes; poetry being her favorite style of writing. She began writing as a sophomore in high school with her high-school newspaper, and she has won several journalistic awards. Her letter is dedicated to David and Christine, because without them the story would not exist. She can be reached at *1motyka36@hotmail.com*. Comments are greatly appreciated.

Dan Mulhausen is a student just graduated from Southridge High in Kennewick, Washington. After his letter was written he had foot surgery in the winter of '98, then came back and competed in his senior year of football and tennis. In football his team made the playoffs for the first time in school history and in tennis he was named team cocaptain. He awaits a response from Notre Dame University. He can be reached by e-mail at *Rudy63@aol.com*.

Amanda Nulman is a recent graduate of Ramapo High School in Spring Valley, New York. She is currently a freshman at Cornell University studying atmospheric science. Amanda would like to thank her family and friends who helped make the project successful and for their endless patience, love and support. She can be reached at *ahn2@cornell.edu*.

Rachel Palmer is a student in Knoxville, Tennessee. She has had poems published in two anthologies, *The Consuming Flame* and *The Mystical Night*. Her letter is dedicated to her true-to-life hero, her father. She can be reached at *Poppy2883@aol.com*.

Amanda L. Poff is a young mother who is aspiring to be a poet. Besides writing, she enjoys nature, music and art. One of her biggest dreams is for her letter to influence teens to cherish their mothers. Mandy can be reached at P.O. Box 32, Princeton, IL 61356.

Caitlin Pollock is a fifteen-year-old aspiring author. She lives in British Columbia, Canada with her parents and older brother. Aside from writing fiction and nonfiction stories, Caitlin is an avid artist, scholar, musician and poet. She is thrilled to have a piece of her writing published in the *Chicken Soup for the Teenage Soul* series. Caitlin can be reached by e-mail at *cjpollock@hotmail.com*.

Michelle Sander is the middle of three girls from a Northern California single-parent home. She graduated with honors from San Ramon Valley High School in June 2000, and began her higher education at the University of California, San Diego in the fall. She can be reached by e-mail at *dmsander@ucsd.edu*.

Tara Sangster is currently a student at the University of Manitoba in Winnipeg, Manitoba. She plans to pursue a degree in arts, majoring in English. Her story is dedicated to all those who see her as "normal." She can be reached at *tarasangster@hotmail.com*.

Stephanie Schultz is a sixteen-year-old junior at Waubonsie Valley High. She resides in Naperville, Illinois, with her parents and brothers. She enjoys working with special-needs children, and is actively involved in her church. Writing has been a way to show her feelings, and she hopes that they will bring inspiration to others. She wants her mom to know how proud she is of her for getting better, and that she loves her.

Erin Seto is a high-school student in Newmarket, Ontario. She is a serious student so school and homework occupy most of her time. When she has spare time she enjoys reading, playing the flute, eating gummy worms and keeping herself busy. "Guy Repellent" was her first writing project. She can be reached by e-mail at *lingseto@enoreo.on.ca*.

Sherry and **Jerry Sharp** have been residents of Virginia for eleven years. Jerry is in retail management and Sherry is a Primary Montessori Directress in the District of Columbia Public Schools. Their daughter, Whitney, was seventeen at the time of her death. She was a senior at Mount Vernon High School in Alexandria, VA, class of 2000. She was a Level 10 USA gymnast and an IB honor student.

Ashley Sims is seventeen and lives in Morro Bay, California. She enjoys writing in her spare time. She feels that writing allows people to get in touch with their emotions and to express them. She hopes that one day she can help make a positive difference in the world.

Meridith A. Spencer is currently a Case Manager at Big Brothers of Mass Bay. She enjoys dancing, being silly and spending time with her family (Ken, Judi, Candice, Kenneth, Keith and Kyle). Although she no longer works at a treatment center, she will forever hold a special place in her heart for the girls of GL, especially ST and KM. She can be reached by e-mail at *mas_letters@hotmail.com*.

Sarah Stillman is a junior in high school who loves writing, reading, and theater. She hopes to enter the field of psychology and has just published her first advice book, *Soul Searching: A Girl's Guide to Finding Herself*. She also enjoys traveling, and hopes to some day study abroad. Sarah can be reached by e-mail at *tupaclovesme@hotmail.com*.

Abbie Stratton is a senior student at Herdman Collegiate in Corner Brook, Newfoundland and she plans to attend Memorial University to study business. This is her second piece published. Her first was a poem in the book, *Songs of the Dawn*. She enjoys writing stories and poetry, and has been doing so for years. She can be reached at *astratton@swgc.mun.ca*.

Renee Tanner lives in Northern Virginia with her parents, sister and her little puppy dog. She enjoys reading, writing and playing basketball.

Laura Glenn Thornhill is pursuing her undergraduate degree at Duke University in Durham, North Carolina. She would like to dedicate this story to the memory of her sister and father, as well to her most cherished friends and the source of all her inspiration: her family. She can be reached by e-mail at *1gt2@duke.edu*.

Jodi Vesterby was raised in Olivia, Minnesota. She currently attends Concordia College in Moorhead, Minnesota, and will graduate in 2001 with a degree in English Education. While attending Concordia, she has been involved in Campus Ministry, Habitat for Humanity and Justice Journeys. She can be reached by e-mail at *pvesterby@thurstongenetics.com*.

Laurel Walker is a public relations student in Nova Scotia, Canada, and will be graduating in June 2001. She hopes that her first piece of published work will inspire others to keep fighting through difficult times. Much love and thanks to family, friends and teachers for their support. Laurel can be reached by e-mail at *laurelw@hotmail.com*.

Nikie Walker is seventeen years old. She lives in Croton, Ohio. She enjoys all sports and is an athletic student trainer at her high school. She is involved in student council and is a class officer. She also volunteers her time to teach younger children about the effects of drugs and alcohol through programs such as Teen Advisors and Prom Promise. She enjoys writing poetry from the heart in her spare time. She is recovering slowly, but she says that the most important thing is that God has been by her side and is allowing her to walk again. She can be reached by e-mail at *babienik@hotmail.com*.

Samantha Yeomans is seventeen years old. She enjoys writing poetry and hanging out with her boyfriend and friends. She hopes that her letter will help people as much as the stories in the *Chicken Soup for the Teenage Soul* books have helped her. You can reach her by e-mail at *ska-girl@home.com*.

Elizabeth Young lives in California and is currently a senior in high school. She writes for her school newspaper and wrote this letter because she wants teenagers to know how fast life can slip away. She can be reached at *blondy712@onebox.com*.

Myrna Yuson is now a third-year student at the University of California, Davis. She is studying exercise science and plans on going to physical therapy school.

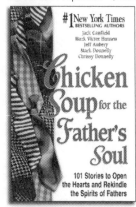

Books for TEENS

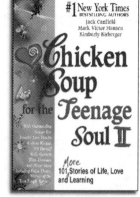

#1 New York Times
BESTSELLING AUTHORS
Jack Canfield
Mark Victor Hansen
Kimberly Kirberger

Chicken Soup for the Teenage Soul II

More 101 Stories of Life, Love and Learning

Code #6161 • Paperback • $12.95

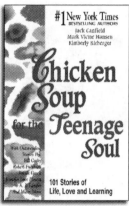

#1 New York Times
BESTSELLING AUTHORS
Jack Canfield
Mark Victor Hansen
Kimberly Kirberger

Chicken Soup for the Teenage Soul

101 Stories of Life, Love and Learning

Code #4630 • Paperback • $12.95

#1 New York Times
BESTSELLER
Jack Canfield
Mark Victor Hansen
Kimberly Kirberger

Chicken Soup for the TEENAGE Soul III

More Stories of Life, Love and Learning

Code #7613 • Paperback • $12.95

#1 New York Times
BESTSELLING AUTHORS
Jack Canfield
Mark Victor Hansen
Kimberly Kirberger
Dan Clark

Chicken Soup for the COLLEGE Soul

Inspiring and Humorous Stories About College

Code #7028 • Paperback • $12.95

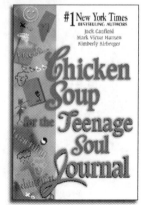

#1 New York Times
BESTSELLING AUTHORS
Jack Canfield
Mark Victor Hansen
Kimberly Kirberger

Chicken Soup for the Teenage Soul Journal

Code #6374 • Paperback • $12.95

Selected titles are also available in hardcover, audiocassette and CD.
Available wherever books are sold.
To order direct: Phone 800.441.5569 • Online www.hci-online.com
Prices do not include shipping and handling. Your response code is CCS.

Bestselling Series

Code #7346 • Paperback • $12.95

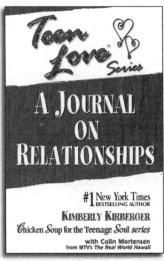

Code #7664 • Paperback • $12.95

Code #8156 • Paperback • $12.95

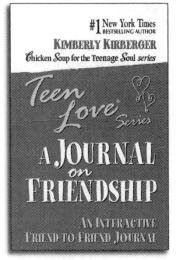

Code #9128 • Paperback • $12.95